Stage Door

The Bristol Hippodrome

100 years

Gerry Parker John Hudson

'Without the Hippodrome the people of Bristol would be deprived of so much that is lovely, for it is a frame which presents the theatrical arts to perfection'

Dame Anna Neagle

First published in 2014 by Redcliffe Press Ltd.
81g Pembroke Road, Bristol BS8 3EA

www.redcliffepress.co.uk
info@redcliffepress.co.uk

text © the authors
cover photograph, design and typesetting © Stephen Morris 2014
set in Garamond 12.5
Printed and bound by Zenith Media

ISBN 978-1-908326-24-9

British Library Cataloguing-in-Publication Data
A catalogue record for this book is available from the British Library

Contents

The cast of *Thanks For The Memories*, 2012

1

A hundred reasons to celebrate

A glittering centenary deserved to be celebrated in style, and The Bristol Hippodrome's hundredth birthday more than fitted the bill as something to get excited about. December 16, 1912 was the night the curtain went up for the first time – but from the beginning of 2012 until deep into 2013 there was a special buzz in the air that captivated performers, staff members and audiences alike.

It is not simply that the grand old lady of St Augustine's Parade has lived on to be at the forefront of entertainment in the city of the twenty-first century after first making her mark in the year of the *Titanic* disaster, the loss of Captain Scott and his brave men and the founding of Britain's first air force, known at that time as the Royal Flying Corps. It is not merely that, in doing so, she has adapted to and sailed through – admittedly rather close to the wind, at times – the competing attractions of the gramophone, movies, radio, talkies, television, video, CDs, DVDs and an explosion of digital delights that must be updated almost by the week. The plain fact is that while the Hippodrome has achieved all this, it has done so in a way that continues to set the pace and expand its horizons.

Most spectacularly, Disney's *The Lion King*, from August 31 to November 17, 2012, rewrote the record books in so many ways. The eleven-week, sell-out run, with tickets priced at up to £75, was the show's first UK production outside London, and the sheer scale of it took even the most seasoned onlookers' breath away. Its cast of forty-eight came from twelve different countries, and while large-scale operations have long been meat and drink to the theatre, thirty-five huge truckloads of scenery and equipment had never been seen around Denmark Street and Gaunts Lane before. In the auditorium, the stalls seating was reconfigured for the very first time for the extraordinary parade of African wildlife that is one of so many spectacular highlights of this show. And while that was a temporary measure, of lasting value to the theatre has been the strengthening of the scenery-bearing grid high above the stage to carry thirty-two tonnes of visual magic.

Early in 2013, another highlight was Cameron Mackintosh's revival of Lionel Bart's *Oliver!*, with Neil Morrisey as Fagin and the young Manx singer Samantha Barks as Nancy. Samantha had come third in Andrew Lloyd Webber's *I'd Do Anything* TV contest to cast the role in the

Tickets to see *The Lion King* go on sale

West End in 2008, but her career had flourished since then and when it came to a long tour beginning in December, 2011, she was the Nancy of choice. She planned to perform the entire run, with its last night at The Bristol Hippodrome in February 2013 – but on April 1, 2012, she took a break from it for the not inconsiderable reason that she had been cast as Eponine in Cameron Mackintosh's big-budget film version of *Les Misérables*. It meant that in the early weeks of 2013 you could see Samantha in both the most high-profile show and high-profile movie in town, which was by no means bad for a twenty-two-year-old. Eventually, she left the show a few days early to join the rest of the *Les Mis* cast at the Oscar ceremony in Los Angeles.

Musicals, new or revived, dominated the Hippodrome's centenary programme, planning for which began three or four years earlier; indeed, musicals have been the big story for much of the twenty-first century, though the diamond anniversary tour of Agatha Christie's *The Mousetrap* and the West End adaptation of television's *Yes, Prime Minister*, with Crispin Redman and Michael Fenton-Stevens, were both virtual sell-outs in May 2013. Matthew Bourne's interpretation of Tchaikovsky's *Sleeping Beauty* and the Scottish Opera and D'Oyly Carte take on *The Pirates Of Penzance* were both apparently traditional pieces with a zesty contemporary tang, but there was a feeling of yesterday once more, welcomed by many, about Sofia National Ballet's *Giselle* and *Swan Lake*, presented in the classical Russian style with a full orchestra in its company of ninety performers.

Perhaps most eclectic of all in the centenary season was the programme of one-night shows, with a breadth of appeal that would have been familiar to the impresarios of old putting together variety and music hall bills a hundred years ago. A touch of mystery? Look no further than Psychic Sally Morgan. Glamour? An evening of West End Burlesque will more than do the trick. Comedy? Step forward Jack Dee and long-time favourite Roy 'Chubby' Brown, whose rude reflections make Max Miller's Blue Book look like the meditations of Thomas Aquinas.

Disney's *The Lion King* – Circle of Life

Music? Motown, The Drifters and The Glenn Miller AAF Orchestra surely tick all the boxes. Shows with which the old-timers might have had more of a problem would be The Dreamboys, 'incredible stripping hunks' whose routines have little in common with Wilson, Keppel and Betty's; and *Hormonal Housewives*, with Toyah Willcox, where the gossip is somewhat riper than when Norman Evans used to chew the fat *Over the Garden Wall*. Besides, how could you fit a word like 'hormonal' on the bill matter?

A show dear to the hearts of General Manager Christiaan de Villiers and his team from the start was the centenary celebration. Ideally it would have been on anniversary day, December 16, 2012, but the somewhat immovable object of the pantomime *Aladdin* put paid to that, and that is why a July slot was chosen. 'At first we were undecided over whether the show should be chronological or a succession of tributes,' says Christiaan. 'We were delighted that Vicki Klein, both a local show producer and at BBC Radio Bristol, agreed to produce our centenary celebration. Vicki had previously produced a theatre seventy-fifth anniversary show, and her first move was to appeal on air for everyone to ring in with their stories. She was inundated;

Samantha Barks as Nancy in *Oliver!* UK Tour, 2012. Photograph: Alastair Muir

the response filled two radio programmes and then they had a meeting here where people could come along and be interviewed. Those who came forward included former staff members and others like the seamstress who had made the stage curtains after the disastrous fire of 1948. The memories formed the basis of the evening, and the cast of 150 from BLOC Productions and Bristol Musical Youth Productions brought it all to life brilliantly. It was a tremendous show.'

Thanks For The Memories skipped effortlessly from opening night in 1912, when Oswald Stoll's vision of the ultimate theatre outside London was at last realised, through two World Wars and once seemingly endless money worries to the vibrant face the 'Hippo' presents to the world today. A special treat was the opening of the dome high above the auditorium in the scene that recalled the devastating fire of 1948. Two cleaners, Doreen and Ethel, played by Sue Donovan and Alison Sutton, gave their insiders' views of the twice-nightly variety acts of the Thirties, both lofty and humble; Sue played Tina, the youngest of the three cleaners, in the 75th anniversary show. 'Now I'm playing the middle one,' she told *The Post*. 'When the 125th anniversary comes around I'll probably play Ethel, the oldest, and complete the hat-trick.' Given her loyalty to BLOC and her devotion to the Hippodrome, she indeed probably will.

A lookalike for the young Archie Leach from Horfield was a reminder that the future Cary Grant was once a call-boy here. Later, Emma Watkins played a wartime usherette who found it hard to come to terms with wearing trousers for work and brandishing a tray that had precious little to offer. The lady who

inspired this section had answered Vicki Klein's appeal and still well remembered the stir caused among her family and fellow workers by those trousers, which were most commonly known as slacks in those days, when worn by women. Then again, before the war she had happy memories of calling out 'Ice cream! Sweets! Cigarettes!' but now sweets were on ration and cigarettes almost impossible to find unless you had a GI boyfriend. As for ice cream, production had ceased because of a shortage of milk, and instead, delicacies such as carrot ice lollies were on offer. With rabbits few and far between among the Hippodrome faithful, demand was not high.

Perhaps humans in the audience were missing something. After all, carrot cake sounded horrible to a lot of us before we tried it. That would certainly have been more palatable than the giant birthday cake brought on at the end of the show, which was not really a cake at all. But it did have a hundred lit candles, and when the entire cast burst into 'Happy birthday, dear Hippo', it was a sentiment with which the audiences at all three sell-out performances concurred heartily

– and with an almost indescribable outpouring of warmth and affection towards the theatre.

A sensation at one performance was an incident in the replaying of the night *The Sound of Music* had been interrupted by a young lady in labour. She had been determined not to miss the show, but started crying out just before the end of the first act. A St John Ambulance volunteer arrived in double-quick time and very soon after she was rushed the short distance to Bristol Royal Infirmary where she produced a fine baby boy, whom she named Jack. As the only member of the backstage staff who answered to that was the stage director Jack Marriott, he always claimed the lad was named after him. In truth, one night there was just as much drama in the re-enactment; Georgina Bond, playing the all-too-expectant mum, was so convincing that the man sitting next to her clicked instantly into professional mode and purred reassuringly: 'Don't worry, my dear. I'm a gynaecologist.'

Songs of successive eras recalled blockbusting musicals from *Guys and Dolls* to *Hair, Joseph And the Amazing Technicolor Dreamcoat* and *Les Misérables*, and the night ended with a roof-raising *There's No Business Like Show Business*. Impossibly schmaltzy and sentimental? Try telling that to anyone who was there – cast, staff and audience alike.

There was a far more intimate feel to the party on anniversary evening, December 16, when staff and cast members past and present, along with others with close ties to the theatre, celebrated after the pantomime's second house. This time there was a resplendent and edible birthday cake, crafted by former staff member David Dunn, and while it was by no means as big as the one paraded with its hundred candles in *Thanks For The Memories*, at least this time it was one to be tucked into. 'It was a very special evening, and because it was so intimate, people who had worked here over the years came back to reminisce and get together,' says Sarah Milne, the Hippodrome's long-serving Press Officer. 'As well as Vicki Klein's Radio Bristol listeners' memories, in July *The Post* appealed for readers' stories about the theatre, and published many of them throughout the summer.' The two appeals also brought in various mementoes, including a programme printed on silk from the first show.

The Hippodrome management's final planning for the centenary had to run in tandem with preparations for the mighty Disney's *The Lion King* and was also hampered by the fact that the theatre's archives are sparse, partly as a result of flooding in the former offices beneath the foyer, and also through sheer indifference to record-keeping in past times. Twice-nightly variety might have brought pleasure to thousands but for those most deeply involved in this transient world of greasepaint, limelight and constant streams of travelling eccentrics coming and going, there was a general assumption that their doings could not possibly be of any interest to future generations.

Fortunately, help has been at hand from various sources. For the 70th anniversary the former journalist Christopher Robinson gathered together a fine array of facts and images for *The History of the Bristol Hippodrome (1912-1982)*, a paperback from the city's Proscenium Publications. Far closer to home today, the Hippodrome's long-serving Box Office Manager, Ian Kennedy, is a magpie who has gathered together a wealth of information, both written and pictorial, which has been invaluable for day-to-day reference.

Coming clean with the Stars

Vicki Klein knew a thing or two when she presented scenes in *Thanks For The Memories* as seen through the eyes of the cleaners, since nobody in the theatre gets closer to the performers than the ladies with the mops and vacs. In some ways they are largely invisible, taking it all in while prima donnas rant and the boys and girls of the chorus bicker and joke. Often from an older generation, they can be friendly and chatty without fear of their motives being misunderstood. And while some staff members keep a respectful distance from the stars, the policy of these girls is that if there's the chance of a photo with Andy Williams, Tommy Steele or Lionel Blair – grab it!

Pat Pearce of Totterdown was a cleaner for twenty years until she was well into her sixties, and cherishes fifteen albums of celebrity snaps. Aged seventy-seven when she talked to *The Post*'s David Clensy in July, 2012, she said: 'We had so much fun. I can't get out of the house much these days – I certainly can't get to the Hippodrome any more – so it means so much to be able to relive all the happy memories.'

Made redundant by Wills, Pat went to the Council House to see if there were any cleaning jobs going, and called in on the spur of the moment when she was passing the Hippodrome: 'I thought it would be unlikely they'd have anything, but I'd always loved the theatre. My aunt and uncle used to take me to variety shows there when I was young. It was a magical place for me. I was amazed when they agreed to take me on. It sounds glamorous, but it was hard work – the hardest work I've ever done. On my first day I heard one of the other girls saying she'd give me until the weekend, so I was determined to stick it out. I was up every weekday at 5am, and 4am on a Sunday, to get into town and start cleaning the theatre from the night before. I would have to clean beneath 508 chairs in the Circle every shift. Sometimes I'd have to clean the stars' dressing rooms.

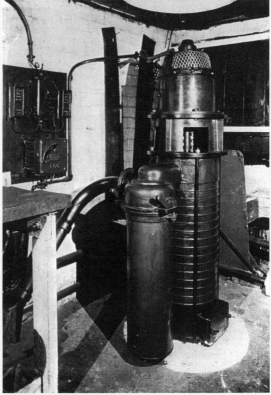

The 1912 vacuum cleaner

1995: Tommy Steele's *What A Show*

Little and Large with Frank Bruno, December 1991. Courtesy *The Post*

'I'd get chatting to them all, and most of them were lovely people. The only one who was really miserable about being photographed was Harry Secombe, which surprised me, but perhaps it was his illness kicking in. I loved Su Pollard. She was so friendly, it was like we'd known each other for years. But my all-time favourite was Albert Finney. He was so sincere. After we'd been photographed I thanked him for posing with me, and he said: "You mustn't thank me, it's for me to thank you." I thought that was so lovely.' Sometimes Pat and her workmates were even invited along to after-show parties: 'I've had a drink with Tommy Steele, enjoyed a chat with Gary Wilmot and one time I even went for a Chinese meal with Frank Bruno and Little and Large. It's the kind of evening you don't forget in a hurry.'

Pat's former colleague Betty Morgan of Lawrence Hill also has special memories of the kindness of Albert Finney and Frank Bruno, as well as Paul Nicholas and Anthony Newley. 'My love affair with the Hippodrome started when I was a teenager and used to wait at the Stage Door to meet the likes of Alicia Markova, Jean Kent, George Formby and Lena Horne,' Betty told *The Post*. 'If I'd known then that I would one day work in this theatre of dreams and attend parties with celebrities, it would have been just too incredible.'

Both ladies were among the last to use the theatre's original central cleaning system. A large vacuum machine was located below the stage and connected via tubes to wall-mounted sockets into which cleaners would plug vacuum hoses. This system lasted more than eighty years, until 1993, when the machine was removed to make way for the raked stage to be levelled. 'It was an extraordinary machine, but we were so used to it, we took it for granted,' said Pat Pearce.

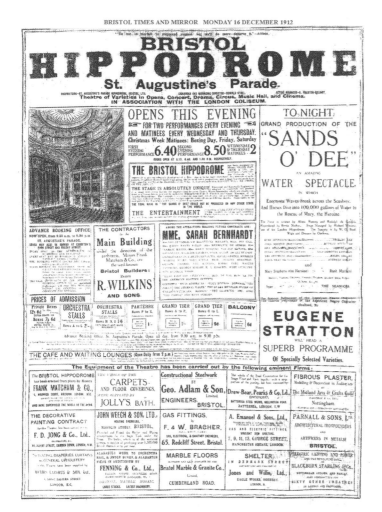

16 December 1912: opening night.
Bristol Times and Mirror

Paintings by Front of House staff members John Ralls (above) and Martin Williamson (right)

Foremost among resources, however, is the website www.hippodromebristol.co.uk, compiled with love and meticulous care by Jonathan Shorney. This is packed with facts, figures and best of all, anecdotes culled from literally thousands of sources, and again its visual content is irresistible. 'It all began when I went to Bristol Central Library to discover the date of a show starring Anthony Newley my mum took me to in the Sixties,' says Jonathan, once an astringent observer of Bristol politics for the *Western Daily Press*. 'It struck me, poring through the daily entertainments listings with their changing fads and fashions, that if a complete record of the Hippodrome's programming had not been compiled, then it should be. It hadn't – and that's how I spent the next two years of my life!' The list has been pure gold to the Hippodrome – but nobody should visit the site without going off at tangents and following wherever its interwoven links might take you in piecing together the Hippodrome's fascinating story. A tip: give yourself a week!

Lasting mementoes of the centenary now adorning the Hippodrome's walls are paintings by two front of house staff, John Ralls and Martin Williamson. John, a great-nephew of Nöel Coward, produced a touching impression of how the theatre appeared in all its glory in 1912. 'I fell in love with the building on first sight,' he told *The Post*. 'I wanted to be the first to produce a historical portrait of Frank Matcham's architectural wonder and provide an insight into Bristol's past. Sadly, today, the pyramid roof and its extraordinary revolving globe have been removed. It was once a landmark for miles around, a magnificent structure of great skill.'

Martin Williamson's humorous and colourful picture shows the theatre's stalls and boxes packed with celebrities associated with it, from its founding fathers Oswald Stoll and Frank Matcham to those who have graced its stage, among them Sarah Bernhardt back in 1913, Laurel and Hardy, Frank Sinatra and Marlene Dietrich. All the great musicals are there and there is even the occasional notable audience member, not least Princess Diana, who once watched her friend Wayne Sleep's *Song and Dance* collaboration with Marti Webb from a box and then memorably danced down the stairs afterwards. Martin, himself an actor and model best known for portraying Isambard Kingdom Brunel at the ss *Great Britain* for several years, told *The Post*: 'This is a Frank Matcham theatre, and you don't get any better than that. I love the Hippodrome, it has great soul. It opened in 1912, at the end of the *Belle Epoch*, and while the world has transformed immeasurably since then, within its walls you enter a building from a more gentle and elegant age – even if it only appeared so on the surface.'

Finally, the appeals for information produced a living link with the first artist ever to tread the 'Hippo' boards. A man in Liverpool phoned to say an ancestor of his was Larola – 'The

1964: the tower is removed

Clever Man With Funny Ways' – who was bottom of the bill on that extraordinary night of December 16, 1912, and as such did indeed set proceedings under way. By the time he was doing this he was a seasoned pro aged forty-four, an acrobatic, plate-juggling Finn originally named Fredrik Horman who worked not only in Britain – including repeat performances at the Hippodrome up until 1922, and a panto stint at Bristol's Prince's Theatre in 1925 – but in the United States, South America and South Africa. Jonathan Shorney's researches have shown that his show-opening stint won praise from the *Bristol Times and Mirror*: 'he did a number of difficult acrobatic feats, which drew the heartiest of applause.' Doubtless even more appreciative was Oswald Stoll; a hapless, tangle-footed, plate-dropping opening act was not on his agenda, and Larola did not let him down. His story is a reminder that throughout its hundred years, it has not by any means been only the stars with their names in lights who have assured the Hippodrome's success.

2

'A type of superior entertainment'

Bristol in the early years of the last century was a city in transition. The masts of small ships still dominated the river Frome's St Augustine's Reach right up to the end of Baldwin Street, and would do so until 1938, but the corporation had been developing the docks at Avonmouth since 1884, and by Edwardian times the streets around the traditional waterfront were looking tired and neglected. Worse than that, in fact, in many cases, particularly the area north of the river bounded by Frogmore Street, Denmark Street and St Augustine's Parade, which had once been part of the grounds of Gaunt's Hospital, a caring place of refuge in medieval times. There had been fields and bowers and fruit groves here – not for nothing was Orchard Street so named when it was developed on some of the land in the early eighteenth century – but all that was a long time ago, and by the time George V was coming to the throne in 1910 this corner of town had become an embarrassment to the city fathers and many of the commercial businesses that were trying to bring respectability to the main streets and the dark underbelly of courts and alleyways beyond them, notably the notorious Hanover Street.

This was the state of play when Mr Oswald Stoll of the London Coliseum applied for a licence 'for music-hall entertainment and cinematograph exhibition at 13 St Augustine's Parade and premises at the rear thereof'. The narrow frontage on to the waterfront had been occupied by two small businesses, the house furnishers Smith and Sons and the chemist Edward Presley, but the jumble of worn-out properties behind was just the kind of unsavoury, insanitary stew the hard-up corporation wished to see swept away, preferably at someone else's expense. Their view was shared by the powerful Society of Merchant Venturers and neighbouring businesses including such big-hitters as Sir George White's Bristol Tramways Company, Canadian Pacific Railways, Pickford's and the sherry and wine importers John Harvey and Sons, who all signed a petition supporting the application. After all, Mr Stoll was known to be an impresario of the utmost responsibility, as well as one with the kind of Midas touch that could only benefit most of the community. In 1898 he had merged his chain of theatres with those of his erstwhile rival Edward Moss to form the all-powerful Stoll-Moss Group, and in the years that followed they had spread their empire – or more precisely, their Empires, Coliseums and Hippodromes – to every community of any size in Britain. Indeed, it is perhaps surprising that it took until

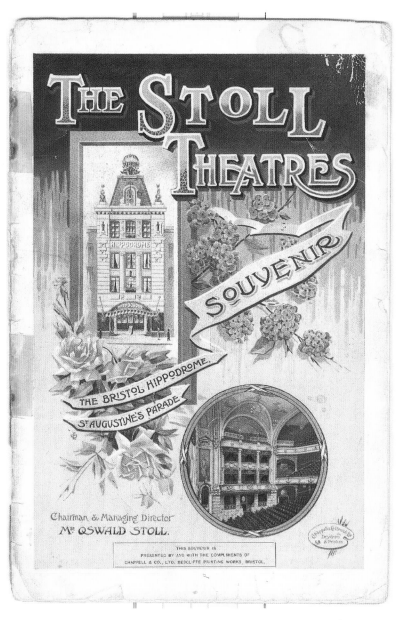

THE STOLL THEATRES

SOUVENIR

THE BRISTOL HIPPODROME,
ST AUGUSTINE'S PARADE

Chairman & Managing Director
Mr OSWALD STOLL.

THIS SOUVENIR IS
PRESENTED BY AND WITH THE COMPLIMENTS OF
CHAPPELL & CO., LTD. REDCLIFFE PRINTING WORKS, BRISTOL.

1910 for Stoll to earmark Bristol, with a population of 357,000, as his next port of call, especially as he had been based no distance away, in Cardiff, for fifteen years from 1890.

Knocking on an open door, then? Not quite. Respectable though Stoll might have been, he was no diplomat, and his widely-reported view that existing Bristol theatres catered only for the lower classes and so would not be adversely affected by his top-of-the-range venture did not stand him in good stead when it came to making friends in the city. 'A type of superior entertainment which would not jeopardise the existing houses,' was one of the ways he put it.

Oswald Stoll

Born Oswald Gray in Melbourne in 1866, Stoll migrated to Britain with his mother after his father had died, and took on his stepfather's name when she remarried. He left school as soon as he was able to help his mother run the Parthenon – no temple to the virgin goddess Athena, this, but a tough old music hall in Liverpool. It was profitable, however, and from that came the ownership of an ever-growing chain of theatres – and a growing sense of responsibility and respectability.

His main competitor was Edward Moss of Moss Empires, and they merged their companies in 1898 with such success that by 1905 their theatres were in almost every major town and city in Britain. At much the time he was opening The Bristol Hippodrome in December, 1912 he was organising the first Royal Command Performance, and his place in the Establishment was sealed when he was knighted by George V in 1919. Stoll continued to spearhead the by then Royal Variety Performances until 1926.

For twenty years, from 1918 to 1938, he ran Stoll Picture Productions, at first from a small studio in Surbiton and from 1923 to 1938 at Cricklewood, in a former pioneering aircraft factory. A legacy that lives on is the Sir Oswald Stoll Foundation, a charity for disabled ex-servicemen in Fulham, not far from his home in Putney. Stoll passed away in 1942, leaving four children – a daughter by his first wife, Harriet, who died in 1902, and three sons by his second wife, Millicent. As for his empire, it was bought by another and far more flamboyant impresario, Prince Littler, who saw the sense in retaining the Stoll name.

Famous for his prim-and-proper ways, some of which were doubtless adopted to emphasize the respectability of his ventures, Stoll grew to accept that not every act that appeared on his bills was as white as the driven snow, and grinned and bore it when the likes of the music hall grande dame Marie Lloyd and the Cheeky Chappie Max Miller peddled their smut and kept his box offices humming. Nevertheless, he would still have his say if he thought an artist had overstepped the mark. 'Mr Stoll, you shouldn't be the manager of a vaudeville theatre, you should be a bishop,' groaned Sophie Tucker, the Last of the Red Hot Mommas.

Oswald Stoll. *Vanity Fair*

This attitude particularly irked the Chute family, formerly of the Theatre Royal in King Street, whose Prince's Theatre in Park Row had a strong pedigree as a 'legit' rather than variety house; they could quote everyone from Sir Henry Irving to the D'Oyly Carte Opera Company among their past attractions, while Horace Livermore, who ran the People's Palace in Baldwin Street, was another angry man. His variety theatre was no distance at all from Stoll's proposed site close to the corner of Denmark Street and St Augustine's Parade, on the other side of the Frome. So Stoll 'wanted to make theatre-going a more respectable pastime, did he?' Livermore snorted. Well, he might be interested to know that the Palace was already patronised not only by the citizens of Bristol, but by even those who lived in Clifton.

In truth, Livermore had a right to be piqued. The music halls of a generation earlier had been rough, boozy and bawdy dens to which respectable men would have hesitated to take their wives, or indeed anybody else's. Stoll had been at the forefront of the emergence of variety, offering entertainment and surroundings with which a middle-class couple, family or group of friends could be proud to be seen, or at least feel comfortable – but just because Stoll-Moss theatres had not previously been in the city, it did not mean that local promoters had not been ignorant of or impervious to this upward trend. Nevertheless, what Stoll was proposing was another league of luxury again, and it was no wonder Livermore feared the worst.

He and the Chutes were joined in their objections by other interested parties including the management of the Empire in Old Market, which was suddenly and somewhat mysteriously being promoted as 'the Empire and Hippodrome', and by Walter de Freece, who was soon to open Bedminster Hippodrome. They had support from the twenty or so other places of entertainment in Bristol in 1911, halls which it was estimated could accommodate audiences of up to forty thousand between them. With traders and residents in the immediate neighbourhood under threat of demolition or disruption organising a petition of some fifteen hundred signatures, there was further well-marshalled opposition ready to object to the application when it came up before the Bristol licensing justices on May 11, 1911.

Stoll told the authorities that he was willing to accept that there would not be cinematograph or secular music performed on Sundays. Persevering with his air of superiority, he argued that he would be engaging artists of a quality that would not normally be seen in Bristol, and that tickets would be bookable in advance to cut down on often fractious queueing before the show. Furthermore, the Hippodrome would not apply for a licence to sell alcohol, a state of affairs that continued for many years.

Not surprisingly, the question of three theatres named the Hippodrome came under con-

'Another league of luxury':
March 1913

sideration, but members of the bench were not unduly concerned by it. The world was a bigger place in those days, and the prospect of one 'Hippo' in Bristol and another across the river in Bedminster did not seem a matter for consternation. As for the theatre in Old Market, it was known universally as the Empire and it came as a surprise to many when it was revealed that it had been registered as the Empire and Hippodrome for some seven or eight years. Stoll said he had not known that, and the magistrates seemed to accept that there was no reason why he should have done. Their view was that his proposal would bring 'a building of a different character entirely' to the city, as well as sweeping away some dark corners from its past, and subject to conditions to which he had no hesitation in agreeing, the future in Bristol was his.

3

A design revolution

Bristol knew and admired Frank Matcham long before he took on the Hippodrome commission; 'one of the prettiest and best-appointed houses in the provinces' had been the *Bristol Times and Mirror*'s verdict on his revamped Prince's Theatre in 1902. Oswald Stoll, of course, knew him even better, since throughout the 1890s he had designed almost all the most significant venues in the Stoll-Moss group, while the London Hippodrome of 1900, Coliseum of 1904 and Palladium of 1910 had seen him reach new heights of splendour, grandeur and innovation. The Coliseum was Stoll's home base, and he made no secret of the fact that he wished Matcham to create the Bristol theatre at least partly in its image. He gave the architect an enormous budget of £30,000, which eventually rose by another two thousand, and price comparison guides solemnly tell us that this is equivalent to around two million pounds today. To which almost of us can say is 'and the rest', for when it comes to property prices, literal comparisons are meaningless. After all, there are streets in Bristol where you would be hard-pressed to buy a house for two million pounds today.

Matcham rose to the challenge, producing a memorable building which impressed equally from its spectacular set-pieces to its minutest details. All the talk in the press was of the tank that could be revealed to the front of the stage to bring into play a hundred thousand gallons of water that could be variously as still as a millpond, choppy with waves, eddying with whirlpools or foaming under a waterfall. Since the tank was of steel, it is hard to see how patrons in the stalls could have seen the drama taking place in it to best effect. True, the floor of the tank was in four sections that could be raised singly or in any combination, but nevertheless, it sounds like one of those situations in which the denizens of the balcony must have felt they had the best seats in the house, for once. So as not to frighten the horses (or actors), the water

The Frank Matcham designs

22

'There is not a stage so constructed in the world': the water tank and lifting platform

was heated to a pleasant eighty degrees Fahrenheit, though it was supplied from a natural spring underneath the theatre. And when things got really splashy, as they did in the first-night *The Sands o' Dee* spectacular, a glass screen fifty feet wide and six feet high could be raised for the benefit of the front stalls (and presumably the orchestra). The rear of the stage also had its moments, with a rising platform some forty feet by thirty-two qualifying as another 'marvel of mechanical skill' in the release Stoll's publicity people sent out to the press: 'There is not a stage so constructed in the world,' they continued, and at some sixty feet deep by eighty wide, it was certainly one of the biggest in Britain.

What struck the audience long before the opening of the curtains, however, was the sheer luxury of their surroundings. Stoll had promised Bristolians something they had never seen before, and he did not let them down. It began as soon as they stepped from the waterfront into the 'grand vestibule' with its advanced booking windows to the left, where the Piano Bar can now be found. 'The office is divided into three distinct compartments,' the press was told, 'with separate counters and assistants for various parts of the house, so that seats can be booked quickly... without the mixing of the different classes...' In fact the Stalls and pre-booked Grand Circle seats could only be accessed from this cosseted environment, with its gleaming

Frank Matcham

"Architect Matcham."

(Frank Matcham)

practice (and marry the daughter) of Jethro Robinson, consulting theatre architect to the Lord Chamberlain's office. Matcham designed some of the most extraordinary public spaces in Britain of his or any other age, not least the London Palladium, Blackpool Tower Ballroom and the County Arcade in Leeds. His many other London theatres included the Hackney and Shepherd's Bush Empires, the Hippodrome, the Victoria Palace and in 1904, for Stoll-Moss, the Coliseum. It was this more than any other factor that prompted Oswald Stoll to call him in for his exciting new project in Bristol, which in the event was Matcham's last major commission.

This was not his first Bristol theatre; in 1902 he had renovated the Prince's in Park Row, and the ventilation dome he had installed there had been considerably refined since then. He had also noted and learned from the tragedy at the Prince's on Boxing Day some thirty years earlier, when eighteen people, mainly children, had been killed in a crush on the slope between the pit and the gallery before a pantomime. In fact safety, not least in lighting and ventilation, was as much a priority to him as creating beautiful spaces. A shadow had been cast over the reputation of Charles J Phipps, the great Victorian theatre architect, by a fire at the Theatre Royal, Exeter that killed a hundred and forty people in 1887. Matcham was determined that no such disaster would sully his CV.

Most of us have an impression of what a lush, plush Edwardian variety hall should look like – and the fact that we do owes almost everything to Frank Matcham (1854-1929). In that golden age of theatre design he was the colossus and between 1890 and 1910 was responsible for more than two hundred of the country's finest, either alone or with two brilliant colleagues he trained, Crewe and Sprague. A Devon man from Newton Abbot, he was apprenticed to a Torquay architect before moving to London in the 1870s to join the

Decoratively, gold moulding, red plush and the use of only the finest materials were his hallmarks, and today an active Frank Matcham Society keeps a watchful eye on the fate of his surviving theatres. These are now invariably cherished and, like The Bristol Hippodrome since 1977, are classed as at least Grade 2 listed by English Heritage. Others, of course, have not fared so well over the years – including the Prince's, which with the nearby Coliseum and so much else perished in the air raids of November 24, 1940.

brass banisters, chandelier and circular ceiling panel depicting the storm scene from *The Tempest*, the last two now sadly gone. But for the Upper Circle brigade and Grand Circle patrons who had not had the foresight to book, their way in was a rather less prepossessing entrance round the corner in Denmark Street.

The advance booking office was an innovation that further set the Hippodrome apart, since most theatres and music halls of the time worked on a first come, first served basis. The grand tier (circle) tea rooms were another, 'daintily decorated and furnished with small tables, chairs, palms and beautiful flowers'. Again, this was an example of advanced thinking, aiming through the café to bring the theatre into the orbit of people's daily lives, as large museums and art galleries began to do some sixty years later and bookshop chains a good deal more recently than that: 'These tea rooms will be made a great feature, for not only are they intended for patrons immediately prior to or during the performances, but are meant for a comfortable and handy rendezvous during the day for friends... The latest periodicals will be found there, as well as material for the writing and dispatch of letters and telegrams.' All this was a world away from the rough-and-tumble of the music halls.

Here and elsewhere in the public spaces, the walls were painted white, where they were not in white and black marble or alabaster. The sumptuous mouldings were in gold leaf (where gold paint must suffice today) and the carpets and soft furnishings, curtains and seating alike, came in a trademark deep red known as *Rose du Barri*. Some might simply see this as Matcham doing as Matcham did, but what made his approach to the Hippodrome unique was his consciousness of that busy seafaring scene on its doorstep and his lavish use of nautical motifs. These take several forms: a profusion of ships' rope and shell mouldings in gilded plaster, richly-coloured fish, ships and lighthouses in stained glass, those brass handrails that could have come from the stateliest liner.

The side balconies, in two tiers of three both left and right of the auditorium, hint of the bowed sterns of galleons. And four large gilded figures of semi-clad goddesses thrusting forward in spectacular figurehead style are reminders of the huge figures of a similarly *déshabillé* Britannia that used to adorn either side of the proscenium arch, to the endless delight of generations of stand-up comics. Morecambe and Wise had great fun with them one time. At the start of their act Ernie reminded Eric that they had agreed not to mention the two figures. 'We won't even look at them,' Eric replied. The seeds were sown, and within minutes even the slightest sideways glance or oblique remark about ships and figureheads had the whole theatre in uproar. That week, Eric from Morecambe and Ernie from Leeds became honorary Bristolians.

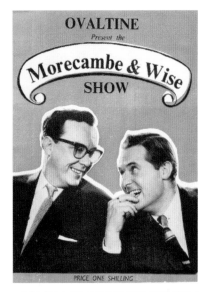

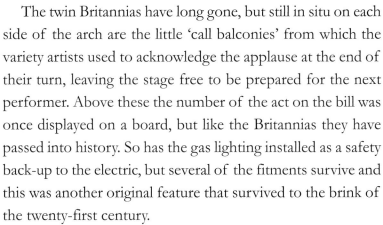

The twin Britannias have long gone, but still in situ on each side of the arch are the little 'call balconies' from which the variety artists used to acknowledge the applause at the end of their turn, leaving the stage free to be prepared for the next performer. Above these the number of the act on the bill was once displayed on a board, but like the Britannias they have passed into history. So has the gas lighting installed as a safety back-up to the electric, but several of the fitments survive and this was another original feature that survived to the brink of the twenty-first century.

Perhaps the greatest headline-grabbing aspect of the auditorium was the central dome that could be slid open to let out the tobacco fumes and let in the cool night air in summer. It is rarely used now – the last time, entirely self-consciously, was as part of the *Thanks For The Memories* centenary show in July 2012. But most people who can look back on regular Hippodrome visits over the past twenty years will recall it fondly, especially on those blessed nights when the stars – and occasionally, unforgettably, the moon – peeped in on the buzzing scene below. To set the record straight: the last time birds encroached into the theatre, two pigeons that wreaked all-too-predictable havoc (much to the amusement of the national media) on the unfortunates in the stalls below them during an English National Ballet performance in 2007 – the dome was

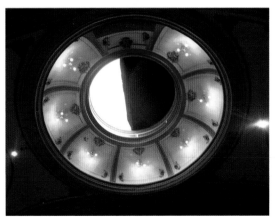

firmly closed. They had found their way in through a considerably smaller hole in the roof.

When first opened, the Hippodrome was capable of holding three thousand with standing in the aisles and the parterre, and the impression gained by most visitors was one of yawning space. One of Matcham's magic tricks, however, at this and other theatres, was to create an air of intimacy in the auditorium when it is viewed from the stage, with the three tiers seeming to huddle round close in an almost friendly, reassuring and supportive manner. 'Like playing in my front room': that sentiment and similar have been expressed countless times by artists through the years, and while non-theatrical folk might take it with a large pinch of salt, to stand looking out from centre stage is to realise that yes, with familiarity and training, the prospect of playing to an audience of two thousand – 1,951 is today's maximum – does not feel quite as daunting as you might have imagined. Still, rather them than me, most of us would conclude.

Four female 'figures of heroic size' supported a revolving dome

What even the outrageously inventive Matcham could do little about was the inconspicuous width of frontage at his disposal on St Augustine's Parade, which had accommodated no more than two modest shop-fronts. He made up for this with a flamboyant Italianate facade with a colourful Art Nouveau-inspired glass canopy, once removed but now happily replicated; and as a crowning glory, a pyramid-shaped tower with four female 'figures of heroic size' supporting a revolving globe some twenty-four feet in circumference with 'HIPPODROME' emblazoned in electric lights. It soon became one of the sights of Bristol, as the Coliseum's globe in London, which inspired it, remains a landmark of the West End. Sadly, the Bristol theatre's owners of fifty years ago found its upkeep beyond their means, and it was taken down in 1964, and if the architect were to revisit the scene, he would doubtless mourn its loss. Venturing beyond the bevel-edged glass doors into the foyer and beyond, however, it is not unreasonable to suppose that his heart would leap at how faithfully and triumphantly the Hippodrome has remained true to the Frank Matcham dream.

◄ 'We won't even look at them': semi-clad goddesses were a gift for the humour of Morecambe and Wise; below: the opening roof from inside and a bird's eye view of the audience

4
Seeing was believing

Even before opening night, the Hippodrome was the star as Oswald Stoll invited a thousand guests 'and their ladies' to tour the theatre, take light refreshments and enjoy a programme of popular music from the resident twenty-six-piece orchestra. We can only surmise what was on the play list, but some of the year's greatest hit tunes – 'Moonlight Bay', 'Waiting For The Robert E Lee', 'When You Were Sweet Sixteen', 'Ragtime Cowboy Joe', 'Who Were You With Last Night?', 'Everybody's Doing It' – give us a tantalising taste of what might have been. Then it was on to the show, and true to his word, on December 16, 1912 Stoll opened with a true headliner, the British-based American minstrel Eugene Stratton. He was a bigger name than had usually been seen in the Bristol halls, and his signature song 'Lily of Laguna' was greeted with wild applause. There was also a full supporting variety bill including, as we have noted, the juggling acrobat Larola, but the real hit of that opening night was the spectacular melodrama *The Sands o' Dee*, chosen expressly to show off Matcham's famous water tank. The audience was thrilled by the sight of Ruth Maitland, as the heroine Mary, being rescued by her lover Rupert Stutfield as he defied Stephen Sorley's evil villain by plunging into the billowing waves on his white horse. The piece might be said to have been based loosely on Charles Kingsley's poem of a similar name; extremely loosely, since in that there was no lover, no villain and no happy ending after Mary had ventured out by the river on a wild night to call her cattle home.

Nevertheless, the Hippodrome's version made a good tale, and the two principal actors were proficient enough to go on to enjoy careers in film. This despite the fact that it took seven minutes for the water to reach poor Miss Maitland's chin, and the much-heralded 'eighty degrees Fahrenheit' seemed to her as big a fiction as everything else about the play. Twice-nightly drenchings on this scale left her with a severe chill, and the rumour-mongers of the day even had it that she died of double pneumonia shortly afterwards. Happily, this was not true, and she was back at the 'Hippo' all of twenty-six years later in an Ivor Novello piece, undeterred by its title, *Crest Of A Wave*.

Many other spectacular productions were to follow: *Wild Australia*, featuring 'Real Australian Bushmen and Women'; *Dick Turpin*, which somewhat incongruously included in its cast Lipin-

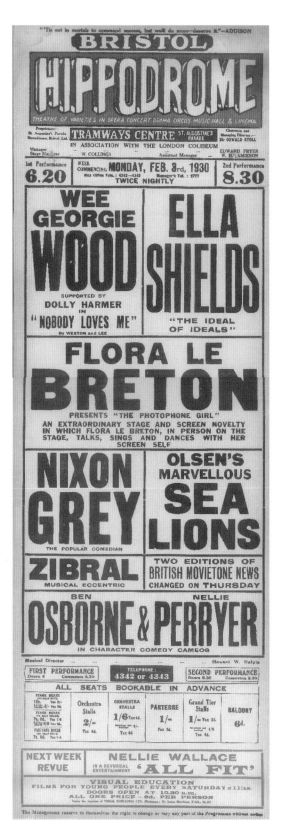

8 February 1930

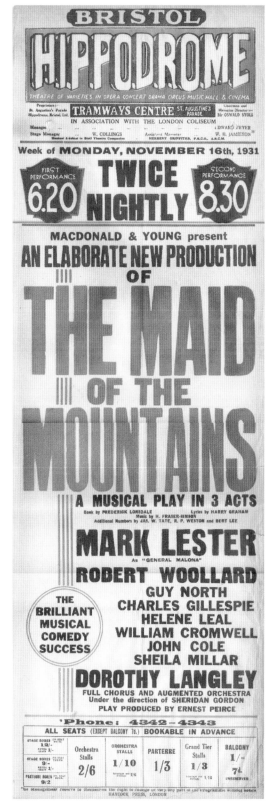

16 November 1931

29

ski's 40 Dog Comedians; and *Cheyenne Days*, complete with 'Cowboys, Lassoers and Riders'. To celebrate its first real Christmas in the theatre the management chose for the 1913-14 holiday period another piece that showed off the tank, this time the ominously named *The Flood*. Bearing in mind that this was the festive season, in the end everything doubtless turned out nice again.

In between these spectaculars, however, there was a bewildering variety of fare. Three days after *The Sands o' Dee* closed, the play *Instincts* was put on with a cast headed by two of the biggest names in early twentieth-century drama, C Aubrey Smith and Lilian Braithwaite. The fifty-year-old Smith had been a renowned cricketer in his youth, having captained England to victory in South Africa in his one and only Test appearance in 1889. Later he was to become Hollywood's favourite elderly English toff in scores of films, and a knighthood in 1944, four years before his death, seemed an apt coda to his career.

Always with an eye on the latest craze, Stoll brought to the Hippodrome one of the first acknowledged film stars, the Vitagraph Girl Florence Turner. She shared the bill with the Royal Carl Rosa Opera Company, as it was then known, and there was another sensational film offering in early June, when a show starring George Formby Senior included the Bioscope Company's coverage of the 1913 Derby, won by *Aboyer* but remembered today only for the drama at Tattenham Corner, when the Suffragette Emily Davison threw herself in front of the king's horse Anmer and suffered fatal injuries. It was one of the first times death, or near-death, had been shown on screen, and it was soon the talk of the town.

The Suffragettes were to the fore again at the Hippodrome from October 27 to November 1, when the great French dramatic icon Sarah Bernhardt was on stage in her most famous role, playing the tragic Marguerite Gautier in Alexandre Dumas's *La Dame aux Camelias*. 'Darling Sarah' was reaching the climax of her celebrated death scene when the moment was shattered from one of the boxes by a group of women loudly demanding the vote, and equal rights with men. Their protest did not find universal support, and several men in the audience heckled them equally loudly. Police reinforcements were sent for and the intruders were unceremoniously taken away to the Bridewell. Sarah Bernhardt was known for having very little patience with any interruption to her performance, and on more than one occasion had halted mid-speech when interrupted by a cough, but there is no record of her feelings on this occasion. As a known supporter of radical causes and the independence of women, perhaps they were more complex than might have been imagined.

Another visitor during 1913 who might have been unamused by the company he was keeping was the comedian WC Fields. This was before he had risen to the heights of starring in the Ziegfeld Follies, with Fanny Brice and Will Rogers, but his acerbic nature was already well known. Famous for not liking children, except possibly to eat, he also took a dim view of performing the comedy juggling act he was doing at that time on the same bill as animals: cue Captain Fred Woodward's Sea Lions.

In November, 1913 the theatre's first manager, N Preston-Hillary, caused a shock by handing in his resignation after less than a year. He obviously left on good terms, however, since a Grand Matinee Benefit was immediately arranged for him, with virtually all those appearing in that week's show taking part. Fred Karno's Mumming Birds company, May Henderson, Woodhouse and Wells, Lumars, Bi-Bo-Bi, Thora and Beth Tate were joined by artists from the Empire theatres in Cardiff, Newport and Bristol, plus some of those who were appearing at the Bedminster Hippodrome. When it came to supporting their own, there really were no people like show people.

The months leading up to the First World War saw very little change in the fare on offer. Spectacles were still making use of that enormous tank of water, while Fred Karno and his merry band were regular visitors – without Charlie Chaplin, who had decamped to Hollywood with the somewhat fanciful ambition of trying to make it big in films. But when war was declared, would there still be a place for the theatre in British life? It was a serious question, but one that was answered soon enough with the realisation that, like never before, there was an insatiable demand for fun, escapism and a dash of good old British jingoism. Cue Dolly Victoria's Troupe of Lady Cyclists. By January 1915, cue a show called *The Contemptible Little Army*, echoing Kaiser Wilhelm's sneering dismissal of Sir John French's British Expeditionary Force. It was greeted with tumultuous applause, and very close behind it came another piece of anti-German nonsense, *Parker catches the K****r*.

Top names from the music hall also began to make their Hippodrome debuts, after their acts had been closely scrutinised by 'The Governor' to make sure they did not include any questionable material. Little Tich, Hetty King, the forces' sweetheart Gertie Gitana, Clarice Mayne, Wilkie Bard and Ella Shields all came to town, along with the Queen of the Halls Marie Lloyd. This last booking marked a complete U-turn by Oswald Stoll, who before he had opened his new theatre had declared that she was just the kind of act who would never play there. Always the pragmatist with an eye to the Box Office, he reached the conclusion that in the more refined atmosphere of a 'proper' theatre Marie's risqué lyrics would be less likely to cause offence, and that her songs were now ideal for the changed times. Whatever the rights and

'Houses literally swept away'

The opening night spectacular, *The Sands o' Dee*, seemed somewhat tame compared with the New Year offering for 1914, *The Flood*. A 'Sensational and Dramatic Spectacle' by Arthur Shirley in which a tarn bursts on to the village of Ripplemere and a 'Huge Rush of 300,000 Gallons of Water' sweeps away all before it. Since the Hippodrome's famous tank held just 100,000 gallons, it seems that there must have been some cunning recycling at play here.

'Trees, Houses and Animals Literally Swept Away. Torrents of Real Rain', the blurb continued, and while we can only wonder how literally to take that 'Literally', 'The Plunging Horses and Bullocks' sound all too probable. For light relief patrons were also offered a Comic Wrestling Match by the Miller Bros, who also played the Lazy Villagers, while the Village Tango by Lottie Stone's Troupe and an Exciting Knuckle Fight also seemed to have their feet on dry land.

The promoters' verdict on the production: 'A perfect triumph of reality'. It seems as if reality shows then had about as much to do with reality as they do now, as was demonstrated in other 'aqua dramas' of the time: intrepid canoeists braved the rapids in 'The Redskin', water burst from the back of the stage to bring down houses in 'Very Soft' and in 'Say When', a submarine surfaced to disgorge a singing sailor. As they do.

Trafalgar Day concert for troops and nurses, 19 October 1917

wrongs of his logical processes, he sensed she would go down a storm, and he was right.

In contrast, and to cater for all tastes, came a visit from the first of many internationally acclaimed dance companies to play the theatre, the Imperial Russian Ballet. The Biograph film company's shorts and news items were now more pressingly relevant than ever, though of course heavily censored. One, which accompanied another flag-waving production, *Kiss Me Sergeant*, showed the First Lord of the Admiralty, Winston Churchill, encouraging factory workers in their war effort. This theme was taken up live on stage by Ben Tillett, the radical

Bristol-born trade union leader who shocked and dismayed many of his brethren by giving the war his wholehearted support. His lecture 'How to Win the War' was given in aid of the Lord Mayor's charities, while Canadian war charities benefited from a Grand Military Concert that featured the Canadian Military Choir and Sextette, along with the Hippodrome's house orchestra under Howard W Galpin. A strange afternoon booking was a Grand Military Torchlight Tattoo, featuring no fewer than a hundred torch bearers. Health and safety? What was that again?

Most of these shows were intended to, and indeed did, boost morale on the home front, and that was certainly the aim of *Money Talks*, which starred Jack Pleasants, one of those bashful, gormless Northern comedians best known for such songs as 'I'm Twenty-one Today' and 'I'm Shy, Mary Ellen, I'm Shy'. It was playing on the day it was announced that hostilities would cease, and every seat and every square inch of standing room was filled that night, with each act being cheered to the rafters. The show over-ran by miles and still nobody wanted to leave; in the end the last few stragglers apparently had to be bodily ejected from the theatre.

Although the war had ended, charity performances at the Hippodrome did not, and just before Christmas 1918 the hugely popular comedian George Robey brought a star-studded company with him to raise money for an endowment fund for elderly and convalescent members of the Sailors' and Firemen's Union, 'fireman' in this case meaning ship's stoker. On the bill was Godfrey Tearle, then still a lieutenant in the Royal Artillery but later another actor who played the quintessential Englishman on Broadway and in Hollywood and was knighted in 1951, close to the end of his long life, for services to drama.

As for Robey, his efforts in raising £500,000 for the seamen's charity more than qualified him for a knighthood, but he refused it, instead accepting a CBE; it was not until a few months before his death in 1954, after he had raised a further two million pounds for charity through the Second World War, that he finally succumbed to the temptation of going down in history as Sir George. Not that gongs and glory meant much to the people of Bristol; but they could see when somebody was doing a grand job, and the Hippodrome's sterling work in helping the war effort sowed the first seeds of the special relationship it was to forge with them. Oswald Stoll had told them he would bring them something special, and now they were beginning to believe him.

5

Animal crackers

With the War to End all Wars behind them and the promise of a land fit for heroes ahead, the British public looked forward to a future of peace and prosperity in which more or less regular trips to variety shows seemed an attainable prospect for many. The Spanish 'flu pandemic of 1918 was a very early warning that Paradise had not yet been attained, and as the Twenties progressed there would be further trials and tribulations for both the people and the entertainment industry. In essence, though, the immediate post-war years were a time – pre-radio, pre-mass cinema-going – when the live show was still king.

GH Elliott, Lancashire-born but America-raised, had inherited Eugene Stratton's crown as king of the black-face minstrels, and he set the decade under way in style at the Hippodrome at the head of a strong variety bill.

Another regular visitor with his 'Selling a Motor Car' and 'Fishing' sketches was Harry Tate. Like many members of his profession he enjoyed a drink or three, but that never seemed to mar his immaculate comic timing. One evening it seemed it might well, when the Stage Manager found him hardly able to walk and swaying in the wings. 'Put me in the boat,' he ordered, and with great trepidation the crew hauled the prop for the fishing sketch to centre stage and plonked Harry in. Needless to say, he went through his routine without a hitch, and his only concession to the state he was in came at the end, when he took his bows still seated in the boat. He knew standing up would be a step too far.

Variety and revue remained the mainstays of the programme for the following years, both drawing the top performers. Nöel Coward's favourite leading lady Gertrude Lawrence was in the cast for the revue *Midnight Frolics* in March, 1921, but well as these shows did at the Box Office, none could match the (male) global evangelist Captain Gipsy Pat Smith, who for three consecutive Sundays in October, 1921 had queues of men surrounding the building. The men-only mass meetings he addressed as part of a Bristol United Free Church campaign always filled the theatre to capacity, and he also did rather well selling his book – an evangelistic phenomenon decades before Billy Graham.

This was a time of animal acts that would be unacceptable to modern audiences. Dozens of circus shows were on tour, and even more performing animals could be found on variety

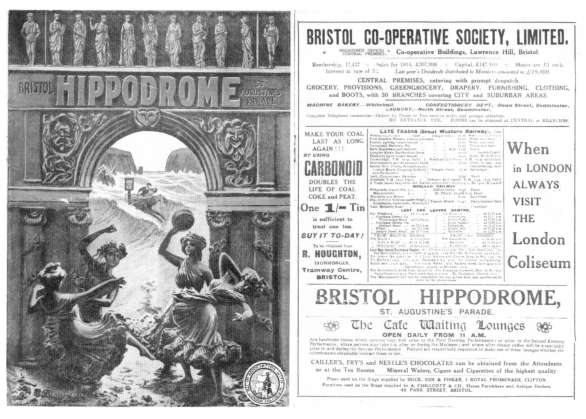

A 1915 programme advertising the Waiting Lounges: 'handsome rooms where patrons may wait prior to the first evening performance... and where dinner coffee will be a speciality'

bills. Captain Woodward's Sea Lions, which had shared the bill with WC Fields before the war, 'sang', played musical instruments and flipped hats and footballs between one another. For a finale, one of them would balance a fish on top of a cane, knock the cane away, catch the fish and eat it. Another favourite was Bostock's Royal Italian Circus, a motley menagerie including an elephant, horses, ponies, monkeys, dogs and even a zebra. Had Frank Matcham really designed his theatre to house a cast like that? Dalmere's Table Circus specialised in smaller animals – cats, dogs, rats, monkeys and doves, while at the opposite end of the scale, the illusionist The Great Como hit town with lions, tigers, another elephant, a boa constrictor, a python, apes, monkeys and a 'White Steed' as his travelling companions. There must have been some tolerant landladies at those infamous theatrical digs.

Three animal performers which most certainly would not be welcome nowadays were a black bear, a boxing kangaroo and a singing duck. Neither would there be many people prepared to pay money – or at least be prepared to admit that they would pay money – to see

Karl Kossmayer and his unrideable mule, an act that was still on the road in the 1960s. Karl would try to ride this creature but would always be thrown off, after which he would offer a cash prize to anyone who could stay on board for a minute. Very occasionally someone with the skill of a rodeo rider would win, but at the Hippodrome there was an incident that was happily never repeated. An American serviceman walked on stage, dazed the poor animal with a ferocious blow to its forehead and then sat on it almost motionless for the allotted minute. Karl might have argued that the tactic was unfair, and disqualified him. But having seen how hard he could punch he simply put it down to experience and paid up, as docile as his mule.

The name 'Hippodrome' comes from the Greek for a horse or chariot race, so it seemed appropriate that at the start of 1921 the show The Circus Queen advertised all the thrills of racing on stage. Alas, the horses were mechanical miniatures, and the Royal Shetland Ponies, which were also on the bill, made it plain that they had no intention of working up a lather. Later in the decade there was actually a greyhound race of sorts on stage, another sign of the management keeping its finger on the pulse of the entertainment business. The new American import of dog racing had first come to Bristol in July, 1927 at Knowle Stadium. It stayed there, along with the Bristol Bulldogs speedway team, until 1960, when the site was sold for housing. Greyhound racing continued at Eastville Stadium until 1997. In the following year, just over a century after it had opened, the stadium was demolished to make way for an IKEA superstore.

There was a particularly strong link between the theatre and the stadium around the time of the Second World War, when Eastville's social manager was Lou Champney. A talented local cricketer, he had always had strong connections with showbiz and would invite almost every celebrity who came to the city to Eastville to present prizes for its frequent charity races. One day Sandy Powell, topping the bill at the Hippodrome, Eric 'Boy' Boon, the British light-weight boxing champion appearing at the Colston Hall and Commander AB Campbell of the BBC's Brains Trust were all on hand. Then there was George Graves, a comic actor who made musical comedy films despite the fact that he could neither sing nor dance. Late in the Second World War he was at the Hippodrome in The Merry Widow – in the role he had played in the original West End production of 1907 – and by this time, it seems, he was taking a rather relaxed approach to his job; a great fan of dog racing, he spent so much time being photographed with Saucy Moon, the winner of the big race, that he was almost late for curtain-up.

6

The Roaring Twenties

Top acts continued to draw huge audiences throughout the 1920s. Gracie Fields arrived in *Mr Tower of London*, and returned twice more during the decade in the show, which gave her her breakthrough in the capital and helped propel her to the heights over the next three decades. Bristol audiences, always quick to spot a talented newcomer, roared their approval of her mixture of comic and popular classic songs, all put over in a voice that prompted some to try to persuade her to train for a career in grand opera. Not that Hippodrome audiences at this time had much of a chance to compare Miss Fields's voice with a genuine classical soprano; they would have to wait for TC Fairbairn's Operatic Stars and the Royal Carl Rosa Opera Company, who between them in two weeks in the autumn of 1931 presented no fewer than thirteen major works. Although the Rosa company had once played the Prince's Theatre, it seemed that at this time Bristol audiences were not at one with such productions, and neither company deemed its visit a success.

A performer who brought a little culture to the variety bills was Bransby Williams, 'The Irving of the Music Halls'. As an actor-manager, comedian and monologist, he had built up an act that fitted neatly into variety. As well as staging scenes from Irving's *The Bells* and Herbert Beerbohm Tree's *Svengali*, he brought a host of Charles Dickens' characters to life in a way that owed something to the writer's own stage performances of the last century. He was a humorous Micawber, a villainous Uriah Heep, a frightening Bill Sikes, a cunning Fagin, while his farewell speech as Sydney Carton facing the guillotine at the end of *A Tale Of Two Cities* left not a dry eye in the house. Hardly a year went by over the next three decades when Bransby Williams was not seen at the Hippodrome.

Another monologist, of a very different kind, was Ernest Hastings. Many of his funny and occasionally poignant tales would find even greater fame when delivered by Stanley Holloway, but in 1922 it was his name that was at the top of the bill along with Eric Blore, a comic actor who was to find worldwide acclaim as a bumbling manservant in the Fred Astaire-Ginger Rogers musicals. Sandy Powell, with his comic ventriloquist act, had to be content with a supporting role, but his day would come.

Later in the decade an American comedy duo who would find worldwide fame provided support for the Irish singer Talbert O'Farrell. George Burns and Gracie Allen's stage act was never as popular with the British public as their later work, and O'Farrell's sentimental *All I Want Is In Ireland* pressed far more buttons than Burns and Allen's precision-timed humour. Somebody else who had to play second fiddle in all three of his visits to Bristol in the twenties was Tommy Handley. It took the Second World War to project him to stardom, with his radio show *It's That Man Again*, satirically abbreviated to the bureaucratic jargon of *ITMA*. Back in 1927, his brilliant sketch 'The Disorderly Room' had to take second place to the Bristol Harmonic Male Voice Choir.

Female silent film fans' hearts were set a-flutter by the enigmatic Japanese-American actor Sussue Hayakawa, who was Full of Eastern Promise decades before the chocolate bars were. *The Samurai*, the play in which he starred at the Hippodrome, is now long forgotten, as are most of his eighty smash-hit movies, but he is remembered by some for his comeback as the honourable Japanese prison camp commandant in *The Bridge on the River Kwai* (1957).

Post-First World War the popular music business was in a changeable mood, and this was reflected in the bands that visited during the 1920s. The Royal Welsh Octette was followed by the Metro Gnomes, while Milton Hayes, who wrote and performed one of the best-known monologues of all time, 'The Green Eye of the Little Yellow God', was accompanied by the John Birmingham Band. Leslie Norman and his Plaza Band came in August 1925 and in November Noni and his Golden Serenaders Jazz Band appeared on a bill with the comedian Dick Henderson, the father of two future frequent visitors to the Hippodrome, Dickie Henderson and his singing sisters the Henderson Twins.

Further contrasting musical styles were highlighted by the St Hilda's Military Band and Jack Hylton and his Kit-Cat Band,

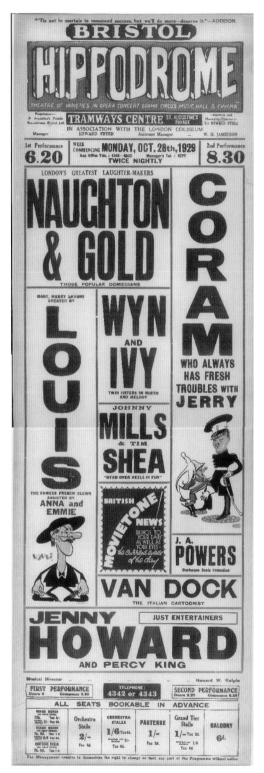

'Say goodnight, Gracie'

George Burns and Gracie Allen, huge in America in the 1930s and later worldwide television stars, were given their radio debut by the BBC in London in 1929, while over here on the variety tour that brought them to the Hippodrome.

They had met in 1922 and first performed together in Newark, New Jersey, scratching together a living in small-town vaudeville theatres. Married in 1926, they moved up a notch when they signed with the Keith-Albee-Orpheum circuit a couple of years later, but the trip to Britain was still a big learning curve for them. George Burns wrote most of the material and in the act that left the Bristol audience only mildly amused, he was the straight man while Gracie played the dizzy, scatterbrained woman who stood her in good stead for the rest of her career. 'Dumb Dora' was a stock character in early vaudeville, but like Morecambe and Wise, the duo eventually succeeded only after they had reversed roles. Early in their career George was the comic, until they realised that even with the feed lines, it was Gracie who was getting the laughs.

The couple had to wait more than twenty years before they really made an impact in this country, with their TV sitcoms of the 1950s. Even then, Gracie did not have the ditzy American housewife field to herself by any means, with Lucille Ball in *I Love Lucy* and Joan Davis in *I Married Joan* putting up strong opposition in the ratings war. Gracie retired after heart problems in the early Sixties and died in 1964, but George had become a showbiz legend before he passed away at the age of a hundred in 1996.

long before Hylton's time as one of the most powerful figures in British show business. In 1926 and 1927, two all-female bands were also popular enough to enjoy prominent billing. The All British Ladies Jazz Band and Ivy Read and her Ladies Band might not have achieved the fame of Ivy Benson's line-up, but they could still blow up quite a storm.

Another regular favourite then and for the next two decades was the Scottish comedian Will Fyffe. He was almost always a guaranteed sell-out, and memories of him were revived forty years later when his piano-playing son Will Fyffe Junior teamed up with Arthur Askey's daughter Anthea for an evening of reminiscences. Fyffe's most popular number was 'I Belong To Glasgow', which he sang dressed as a scruffy labourer. His son told the tale of the night his father and a friend, returning from a fishing holiday in Scotland, stopped off in a town in the North and after dinner spotted a notice offering a £5 prize to whoever could sing 'I Belong To Glasgow' most like Will Fyffe. 'They'll never recognise you,' said the friend. 'Go for it.' So go for it Will did – and came third.

7

The silver screen years

By the late Twenties, the rise of the silent cinema was throwing live theatre managements all over the world into crisis mode, while the launch of BBC radio nationally in 1927 was another potential hazard. All this was nothing, however, compared with the impact of the talkies. Almost overnight everyone wanted to go to the pictures to see the new romantic heroes and heroines, and the all-singing, all-dancing spectaculars that pushed production values to undreamed-of heights. An extra complication as the Thirties wore on was the toll both radio and the cinema took on the brightest talents in variety. Twice-nightly shows six days a week, with the Sunday spent decamping from one town to another, added up to sheer hard graft. For the jugglers and acrobats and animal trainers, the bread-and-butter 'spesh' acts, reaching an audience of maybe twelve thousand a week all over the country was a decent and sometimes exciting way of earning a living. But what of the likes of Will Fyffe, Gracie Fields, Will Hay, George Robey? Suddenly they could earn more and reach millions through the radio, film and recording studios of London, and Tuesday matinees at the Sunderland Empire or even the Bristol Hippodrome were not quite so appealing any more.

Oddly, it was the Hippodrome, rather than one of the purpose-built cinemas springing up all over the city, that showed the first full-length talkie seen in Bristol. *This is Heaven* (1929) was a strange hybrid, released in both silent and sound versions, though even the latter was largely silent with three talking sections inserted. Its stars were the Hungarian Vilma Bánky and the Texan James Hall, and though he had a big hit at much the same time with Howard Hughes's *Hell's Angels*, with Jean Harlow, the talkies spelled the end for both of them.

Horace Livermore, fast losing his battle with the Hippodrome for theatre audiences, had long since turned his People's Palace into a cinema, while Bedminster Hippodrome's threat as a live venue was snuffed out when Stoll acquired it and turned it, too, into a picture house. Despite this, the challenge of the film industry was such that by the end of the 1920s some unusual performers were brought in for novelty value, not least the Australian Annette Kellerman, who bravely dipped her toe into Frank Matcham's giant on-stage tank. Allegedly the first woman to wear a body-hugging one-piece bathing suit on stage or in films, she is often credited for inventing the sport of synchronised swimming, after a water ballet in a glass tank at the

New York Hippodrome. But that had been some twenty years earlier, in 1907, so, now in her early forties, it is questionable how well she fared on artistic merit in her Bristol show. Neither was there anything very eyebrow-raising about her supporting cast, headed by Ernest Hastings with yet more of his endless monologues.

Another exotic was the handsome – indeed 'Gorgeous' – Frenchman Georges Carpentier, former war hero and European and world light-heavyweight boxing champion turned schmoozy gallic song-and-dance man. In March 1929 he shared the bill with the petite American Frances Day, who would go on to enjoy a glittering decade of stardom on film and in the West End. It had been back in 1921 that Carpentier – not only 'Gorgeous' but 'The Orchid Man' – had tried his luck against the world heavyweight champion Jack Dempsey in the first boxing match to generate a million dollars. Although badly beaten that day in Jersey City, he had taken a large slice of that huge purse home with him to France – and forged a lasting friendship with Dempsey.

The Hippodrome battled on for a further three years before it gave way to financial pressures and converted full-time to cinema, and experimented in various ways to try to stem the tide. In January 1931 it flirted with a week of pantomime for the first time; up until then Stoll had always left the seasonal show field clear for the Prince's, which had a big reputation in the panto world, but *Dick Whittington And His Cat* gave him a pleasant surprise with a sell-out at every performance. Audiences particularly loved the principal boy, Peggy Rhodes, and she was back the following winter with *Robinson Crusoe*, again for just a week over Christmas. Then after a short visit from *Les Femmes de Paris*, another panto, *Babes In The Wood*, followed

The first talkie in Bristol, Banky's 1929 *This is Heaven*

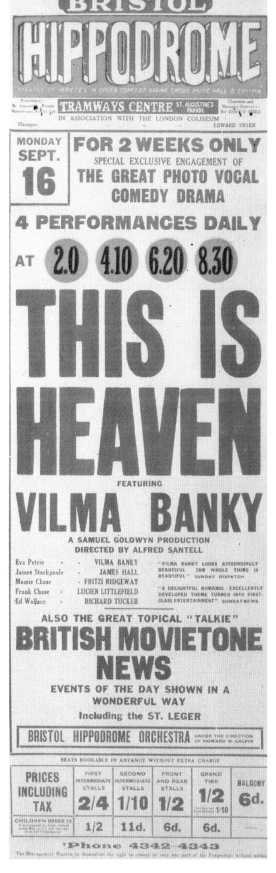

in the middle of January, 1932, with a strong juvenile cast that included babies Joan and Yvonne as the Babes, Ida's 20 Little Dancers and 12 Corona Kiddies. Gus Elton and James Lomas headed the bill. W C Fields did not. Already, though, there had been hints of things to come. Educational films for young people were being shown regularly at the Hippodrome, as well as coverage of big sporting events such as the 1930 Grand National. Just as exciting must have been pictures of the British R100 airship arriving in Montreal after its epic flight across the Atlantic, and newsreel footage of Britain's third consecutive victory in the Schneider Trophy air race; the Supermarine aircraft that secured the trophy would be developed by its designer RJ Mitchell into the RAF's most celebrated Second World War fighter, the Spitfire. Boxing matches were another favourite – Scott v. Sharkey, Carnera 'The Ambling Alp' v. Meen, and Scott v. Gains – which shared the bill with as strong a gathering of comedians as ever graced the Hippodrome in one evening – Will Hay, Max Miller and Max Wall. Not to mention Leslie Pearce and his Singing Hussars.

The first edition of the *Bristol Evening Post*, which hit the streets on Monday April 18, 1932, tells us much about where entertainment was heading in the city. Leading the What's On entries that day was a modest advertisement for the Hippodrome show *The Follies of Buenos Aires,* a 'Delightful and Original' production starring Queenie May. Immediately below it was a far bigger listing for the Stoll Picture Theatre, previously the Bedminster Hippodrome, which was showing Marlene Dietrich in *Dishonoured*. Ten other talkies were advertised, including Elissa Landi and Lionel Barrymore in *The Yellow Passport* at the New Palace. The only other theatre shows noted were at the Prince's, which was presenting the play *The Queen's Husband*, and the Little Theatre's comedy *Petticoat Influence*. This new evening paper would play an important part in the future of the Hippodrome, keeping it constantly in the public eye and helping stimulate support for it after the disastrous fire of 1948 and in the great financial crises of the 1960s and '70s.

And then, on October 15, 1932, came the end of live performances at the Hippodrome for ever – or so it seemed to those in the audience that night, and doubtless to many on stage and backstage as well. Why should it not have been? It was going over to cinema full-time, cinema was the state-of-the-art new entertainment phenomenon. End of story – surely? It was a cabaret that the theatre set before its patrons that night, starring the violinist Jan Ralfini with his jazzy dance band. A full house greeted them, and every act – Ike Freedman, Lee Cash, Bob Lloyd and Betty Hill, Neville Bishop and Freddie Bamberger, Gaby and the Six Gibson Dancers and the rest – was cheered to the rafters. Those cheers were mixed with boos and

Magnificent Marlene

A massive movie hit at the Hippodrome in April, 1933 was *Blonde Venus*, starring the theatre's former call boy Archie Leach (Cary Grant) and Marlene Dietrich in her third Hollywood role. Directed by her mentor Josef Von Sternberg, her contribution to the eight-minute 'Hot Voodoo' jazz sequence caused a sensation. Thirty-two years later she was to cause as big a stir, though for very different reasons, when she appeared live at the theatre for a week in September, 1965. Exquisitely gowned and coiffured, she commanded the stage from the start and oozed glamour and sophistication as she sang, or rather talked her way through, 'Falling in Love Again' from *The Blue Angel*, 'See What the Boys in the Backroom will Have', which she had introduced in the spoof Western *Destry Rides Again*, and the song the British Eighth Army stole from Rommel's Afrikakorps, 'Lili Marlene': all were received in an atmosphere of nostalgia and admiration. She also told fascinating stories about the Golden Age of Hollywood, despite the fact that she had always claimed that her work and the people she had met there were lightweight. The orchestra that backed her

and her skilled accompanist William Blezard was hardly noticed by an audience dazzled by a true superstar. Blezard spent twenty years playing and writing songs for a very different star, the wonderfully understated Joyce Grenfell, and it says much for his versatility that he could find favour with these contrasting talents. When Marlene left the theatre she found Denmark Street crowded with fans, and for a moment it looked as if she might have difficulty in reaching the limousine waiting to take her back to the Grand Hotel in Broad Street. Then, as one onlooker put it, she did not need any minders to clear a pathway for her; she simply swept forward and the crowd parted like the Red Sea for her to step into her car.

That is not quite as the former constable MB Cross of St Annes, Bristol, remembers it. 'I was detailed to wait outside the Stage Door in Denmark Street to make sure that when Marlene came out there were no anti-German protests,' he told *The Post* in 2012, 'so for the whole week I would accompany her from the Stage Door to the restaurant opposite, where she had her evening meal. There were no problems and on the Saturday night she came out as usual, with a few dozen people hoping they could get her autograph. She put her hand up and asked for quiet and then said: "I would like to thank this lovely officer for looking after me" – and then she kissed me!'

Nöel Coward

Margaret Lockwood, signed for the
Hippodrome's Sydney Phasey

catcalls for the management, however, and appeals for order met with little response. It was long after the final curtain came down that the last of the audience left, and as on the day the end of the First World War was announced, some had to be forcibly ejected from the building.

With eyes fixed firmly on the cash registers, the conversion from theatre to cinema took only a week, and seven days after Jan Ralfini and his boys had climbed aboard their band bus, billboards proclaiming the arrival of *Congorilla*, coupled with *Mystery Ranch* had sprung up outside the Hippodrome. For the rest of 1932 the on-screen fare was distinctly standard, though the year ended with a popular new version of *Rebecca of Sunnybrook Farm*, starring Marian Nixon and Ralph Bellamy, and with his connections in the film industry, Stoll did his best to pull out some plums along the way. Spectacular productions had been a staple diet at the Hippodrome from the outset, and after a steady start, this policy was reflected in a choice of films which took in everything from Cecil B DeMille's *The Sign of the Cross* to *King Kong*, Nöel Coward's homage to imperial Britain, *Cavalcade*, *The Three Musketeers* and *Victoria the Great*.

Occasionally, to the delight of the fans, a star of the picture would appear in person. John Loader came in 1935 to boost the Box Office for *Lorna Doone*, in which he played John Ridd. That said, the public would probably have preferred to have seen Margaret Lockwood, who made her film debut in RD Blackmore's *Romance of Exmoor* and went on to become for a time the biggest star in British films. Later she would appear many times at the Hippodrome, flying through the air as Peter Pan, playing Amanda, the most sophisticated of ladies in Nöel Coward's *Private Lives*, Eliza in *Pygmalion* and in several Agatha Christie thrillers. In those pre-television days news that part of the coronation of George VI and Queen Elizabeth in May, 1937 was to be shown in glorious Technicolor caused great excitement. In fact after the colour input a further twenty minutes of the service was screened in black and white, but it was so popular that it was brought back the following week.

And yet... as the six years of cinema at the Hippodrome ticked by, there was a growing feeling that it did not seem quite right. The auditorium was huge, with not far short of two thou-

From the scrapbook: John Mills, Flora Robson, Randolph
Sutton and Flanagan and Allen

sand seats, and it called for something special from Hollywood to fill those to anything like
capacity every night. Serving as a mere cinema seemed somehow to be selling it short, as indeed
many had felt from the start. Besides, although war was still two years away, by this time it was
already feeling inevitable in the eyes of all but the most eternal of optimists, and the great
hall's role in boosting the morale of the people of Bristol during the conflict that had ended
less than twenty years previously was still clear in the memory. By the high summer of 1937
the time was right for the Hippodrome to go live once more. So with a routine piece of Hollywood hokum – the three-year-old *Manhattan Melodrama*, starring Clark Gable, William Powell
and Myrna Loy – it was back to the business it knew best.

8

Going live again

As when it converted to film, it took just a week to restore the Hippodrome to being a live venue again, reopening on August Bank Holiday Monday. 'Who Says Variety Is Dead?' asked the banner headline in the *Evening Post* – a useful piece of publicity but also a reminder that some saw this as a brave (or foolish) defiance of current trends. In London the guv'nor himself, Sir Oswald Stoll, personally vetted the opening night acts and his Regional Manager John Christie, later to take over at the Hippodrome, was on hand to ensure that all ran smoothly, Top of the bill was the Scots actress Renée Houston, who at that time was touring with a comedy routine along with her third husband, Donald Stewart, but would later become a stock 'battleaxe' in British films. It was not the strongest line-up – *The Desert Song* tenor Harry Welchman, the musical comic Joe Termini, the droll Billy Russell and then a cast that sounds like a parody of a stock variety bill: Basyl, Raphonso and Page, Arthur Pond, Beam's Five Acromites, Sam Linfield... Probably none of these worthies would have chosen to reopen an inland theatre on the big bank holiday of the summer, but the warmth of the reception each of them enjoyed convinced everyone that Bristol was delighted to have its much-loved 'Hippo' back in the business of live theatre.

Some big acts followed – George Robey, Elsie and Doris Waters, Nellie Wallace, Stanley Holloway, the urbane Weston Brothers – and the *Britain's Got Talent* of the day, *Carroll Levis and his BBC Discoveries*, pulled in a host of eager young talent in September, 1938. Sadly, nobody on the bill was able to emulate the likes of *Discoveries'* Nicholas Parsons, Bert Weedon and Terry Hall and Lenny the Lion and make it to the top. The personal appearance that caused the biggest stir in Bristol in 1939 was that of the American cowboy star Tom Mix. A crack shot and genuinely a former cowpoke, he had won national riding and roping contests, and between 1909 and 1935 had made 291 films, almost all Westerns and all but nine of them silents. By the time he came to Bristol more glamorous young stars had taken on his mantle, but that did not seem to make the slightest difference to the crowds that lined the streets and brought the traffic to a standstill as he made his way from Temple Meads to the theatre on his equally famous white horse, Tony. In truth, Tom was an old hand at this, on two continents; talk to elderly American men today and a memory you will hear time and again is of the day

Tom Mix rides into town

Tom Mix hit town and rode Tony up the town hall steps. No wonder there was widespread sadness when the old boy died in a car accident in Arizona just a year after his Bristol triumph.

An odd episode, the summer of 1939, in more ways than one. At the height of it, in June and July, there were not enough variety acts to go around, and for a brief, unheralded spell it was even back to showing movies again – albeit a blockbuster in the case of Cecil B DeMille's classic *The Plainsman*, in which Gary Cooper and Jean Arthur led the cast in a highly fictionalised account of the relationship between Wild Bill Hickok, Calamity Jane, Buffalo Bill and General Custer. By the beginning of August it was back to variety again, headed by one of the few female comedy duos to make it to the top, Ethel Revnell and Gracie West. All very well: but then came September 3, 1939.

As with the beginning of the First World War, the Government closed all theatres, along with concert halls, racecourses and greyhound tracks. The 1939-40 league football season was abandoned. And as before, once the situation had been assessed, it was back to, as near as possible, business as usual. In the Hippodrome's case, this was a visit by Sandy Powell, one of the fiercest opponents of the closures, and before the year's end the comedian Billy Bennett, the musical comedy star Evelyn Laye and the perennial schoolboy Wee Georgie Wood had all appeared for a week's run. On December 10, 1939, came one of those nights the 'Hippo' did best in both World Wars, an All-Star Variety Concert in aid of Bristol's Own Fund, attended by the Lord Mayor and Sheriff. It starred big names from every quarter of showbiz: Tommy Handley and his *ITMA* cohorts Horace Percival, Fred Yule and Jack Train, Dick Bentley, Jack Hylton and his Band, the bandleader Billy Ternent, the future Dixon of Dock Green Jack Warner, Anne Ziegler, Suzette Tarri, Phil Green and a good many more. Even David Burnaby chipped in with *Keep on Sewing, Mrs Sew and Sew*, an early wartime morale-booster – and, of course, there was the Bristol Aeroplane Band. One of this number, Phil Green, returned fourteen years later as the musical director of the 1953 production of *Guys and Dolls*, the first big American spectacular to have its pre-London run at the Hippodrome; it was not long before he was reminiscing about that emotional night.

All this action came in the period known as the Phoney War, before the collapse of the British Expeditionary Force and its allies in France and the rescue of many of them from the beaches of Dunkirk in May, 1940. The Battle of Britain that followed brought the war starkly on to the Home Front, and Bristol was to become the fifth most bombed city in England. In all, it suffered seventy-seven air raids, six of them classified as major, during which nearly thirteen hundred people were killed and a similar number seriously injured. The night everyone remembers is November 2, 1940, when ten thousand tons of high explosives and five thousand incendiary bombs were dropped on and around the old heart of the city, destroying much of it. The Hippodrome survived that night, as did its sister theatre, the Prince's, but for the latter it was not for long. Looking to drop the few bombs he had left on the City Docks before heading for home, a Luftwaffe pilot missed his aim and destroyed both the Prince's and the Coliseum that stood opposite it in Park Row. At the time, the Prince's was considered by the London management to be the premier Stoll-Moss theatre in Bristol, and it had even been rumoured that the Hippodrome might close in its favour. That threat remained, and after the war inquiries were made about the possibility of rebuilding the Prince's and converting the Hippodrome into offices and shops. By this time, however, local and national authorities saw the rebuilding of places of entertainment as a low priority for scarce construction materials, and the project was dropped, never to be resurrected.

Although not seriously damaged, the Hippodrome had to cancel two bookings towards the end of 1940. A visit from Tommy Trinder for the last week of November was postponed, though he made it in the following year with a show named after his catchphrase, 'You Lucky People'; Harry Korris, the man who fronted another wartime radio favourite, *Happidrome*, managed to complete the next week's run with 'Two-Ton' Tessie O'Shea; then the bombing was so severe that no more shows were booked until the week before Christmas, but that was the last time enemy action brought the complete cancellation of a Hippodrome show. When it reopened there was no time to arrange a pantomime so it was a variety bill headed by Vic Oliver that played the week before Christmas, and another, starring the romantic duettists Anne Ziegler and Webster Booth and the 'drunk' (in real life teetotal) comedian Jimmy James, that took over on December 30. There were nights, of course, when it was thought prudent

Don't call me Syd

Even when conducting community singing under the stage, Sydney Phasey would still be immaculately turned out in white tie and tails. None of the audience and few of the theatre staff knew that when he arrived one evening he was dressed in virtually the only clothes he possessed. The night before, while he was at the theatre, his home had been destroyed and after spending most of the day searching the rubble, he found that most of his wardrobe had been lost. Despite this, there was not a hair out of place or a hint of distress when he raised his baton for the first-house overture that evening, and it is little wonder that when reporting on the fire of 1948, the local press noted that Mr Phasey's dress suit had been among the survivors.

The Hippodrome management team in the forties, left to right: Cyril Howe Assistant Manager, Albert (Goodie) Good Stage Manager, George Higgs District Manager, and Sydney Phasey Musical Director.

1948 Management Team: Cyril Howe, Assistant Manager; Albert (Goodie) Good, Stage Manager; George Higgs, District Manager; Sydney Phasey, Musical Director

Nobody called him anything but Sydney, but one night somebody got away with 'Syd'. A full house had been in their seats for some time before news arrived that the 'King and Queen of Broadway Drama', Alfred Lunt and Lynne Fontanne, had been delayed after a serious rail accident at Paddington. The audience began to get restless, but the day was saved when one of them shouted: 'Give us Syd and his orchestra and we'll be all right!' For once Mr Phasey overlooked the indignity, and he and his players responded by entertaining the crowd for well over an hour with popular songs and light classics. When Lunt and Fontanne eventually arrived for Robert E Sherwood's play *There Shall Be No Night*, they were given a warm reception by a contented audience.

Most major theatres had an in-house orchestra, but few could match the consistent quality of the Hippodrome's. Musicians as diverse as Ziegler and Booth, the ukulele-playing Tessie O'Shea and the great Austrian tenor Richard Tauber all spoke warmly of Sydney Phasey and his orchestra. Tauber was seen by most critics as the finest tenor of the twentieth century after Caruso, but in the spirit of many more recent operatic stars he was keen to share his gift with a wider audience, and when he brought his hit operetta *Old Chelsea* to the Hippodrome, he sent them all home humming *You are my Heart's Delight*. Many a comedian was also grateful to the orchestra for playing stooge and making silly noises for their routines. Sometimes it was the drummer who had to hit a loud note or blow a raspberry at the right moment, but more often than not it was the tall, slim, lugubrious bass player who was the target of their comedy. He was never known even to smile, so it became a running battle between him and the comic. Many tried, but gave up without even the comfort of a sheepish grin to show some of their gags had got through to him.

Sydney Phasey was a great collector of photographs signed and dedicated by the stars with whom he worked, and his albums are now a vital source of material for local theatre historians. In truth, there is the odd 'Syd' in there, and, whisper it not, even the occasional 'Sid', but doubtless he grinned and bore it when in the presence of showbiz royalty. Sadly, like everyone else, he was out of a job at the Hippodrome when the fire struck, despite the saving of his suit. He answered the call of his friend the maverick theatre owner Freddie Butterworth to switch to the Empire in Old Market, and the appointment was all over the newspapers. Sadly, the move failed to boost flagging attendances and Sydney, close enough to Butterworth to have been a witness at his wedding, was given his marching orders after just eight weeks.

to clear the theatre while an air raid was in progress, and then the portly figure of the manager George A Higgs, would invite the audience either go to one of the shelters around the Centre or join him and Sydney Phasey, the theatre's musical director, under the stage for some community singing. Often they would be joined by some of the acts, and an impromptu show would start. Sometimes the audience down there would be treated to a show almost as long as the one they were missing.

The abandonment of the 1940 panto was a disappointment for children in particular, since with the Prince's Theatre destroyed they were left with no show. The previous year they had enjoyed Dan Leno Junior in *Mother Goose* and were to have another taste of that panto at the end of 1941, this time with the finest Dame of his generation, George Lacy, in the title role. In all, Lacy played in more than sixty pantos in a career spanning from 1929 to 1984 – but all this was of no comfort to the deprived kids of 1940. Although they had come late to pantomime, once under way, the Hippodrome management realised the value of these seasonal shows, and they played a big part in the survival of the theatre during the financially difficult wartime and post-war years. There was a real coup in 1942 when George Robey headed the cast of *Robinson Crusoe*. 'The Prime Minister of Mirth' was the most prestigious comedian in the land; this does not, of course, imply that he was the funniest, but like many comics he was also a wonderful actor who had played Sancho Panza in two film versions of *Don Quixote* before Laurence Olivier chose him to be Falstaff in his spectacular, star-studded version of *Henry V* in 1944. Those who saw him in *Robinson Crusoe* did not doubt that he invested as much into it as he did into the Shakespearian role.

For the next two years the pantomime cast was led by Duggie Wakefield, another of those flatcap, gormless Northern comics whose film career was not harmed at all by the fact that he was Gracie Fields's brother-in-law; and in the spotlight in 1945 and on into peacetime in 1946 was Nita Croft, who became a favourite principal boy with Bristol audiences and was a regular leading lady in touring productions of old musical comedy favourites such as *White Horse Inn*. In 1945 she shared top billing with the Crazy Gang's 'Monsewer' Eddie Gray and the next year, in *Sleeping Beauty*, she was partnered by another popular comedian, Freddie Forbes.

In among the regular variety bills, drama was a strong feature of wartime offerings, none more so than when the stage version of Graham Greene's *Brighton Rock* came to town in 1943, led by a teenage Richard Attenborough and featuring several who would go on to play in the much-acclaimed film, William 'Billy' Hartnell, Hermione Baddeley and Harcourt Williams among them. Dulcie Gray was another impressive figure, but some in the audience found this evocation of inter-war gang warfare rather too dark and harrowing. Bearing in mind what they had been going through in real life not long before, it is a reminder of the abiding power of the theatre.

Then, in May, 1945 it fell to George Higgs, the Hippodrome's longest-serving manager, to have the pleasure and privilege of interrupting a performance of the comedy *Arsenic And Old Lace* to explain to the audience why they could hear church bells ringing outside: the war was over. In fact only the proverbial Man from Mars would have entered the theatre an hour or so earlier not knowing that such an announcement was imminent. But now it was official – and the audience raised the roof with their cheers of joy and relief.

9

The Hippodrome in flames

Call it ironic, call it tragic, but the drama of February 16, 1948 – the war safely over and the recent marriage of the King's elder daughter a welcome beacon of hope in a still grey and austere world – threatened the existence of the Hippodrome more than any other single calamity in its hundred years. It was a week before the end of the panto *Babes in the Wood*, starring Arthur 'Old Mother Riley' Lucan and his wife Kitty McShane, and they had been playing to packed houses since Christmas Eve. It was at that time in a run when everybody, performers and backstage crew alike, knows exactly what they are doing, and on a good day you could almost feel the show could run itself. February 16, 1948 was not a good day.

Early afternoon, about one o'clock, and most of the guys were out for lunch. Seemingly out of the blue, one of them still there caught someting out of the corner of his eye and looked again to see fire. Fire is not good anywhere, but particularly in the stage area of a theatre more than sixty years ago, when curtains and gauze and thick, gaudy paint on wooden scenery made the whole working space as combustible as a tinder box. The alarm was raised, but within what seemed like seconds the whole of the stage was ablaze, with flames leaping thirty feet high. Firefighters from a couple of minutes away in Rupert Street and from the fire float *Pyronaut*, at the head of St Augustine's Reach, managed to contain the blaze at the orchestra pit, though not enough to save the famous old water tank, which in truth would have faced health and safety concerns over the next few years, anyway. Although Matcham's magnificent auditorium suffered no direct fire or heat damage, smoke and water left it in a sorry state. A major contribution to the operation was the opening of the dome, which made conditions more tolerable for those inside and allowed the firemen access for their hoses from above. Understandably, whether or not quite so much water needed to be pumped into the circle and stalls did not seem a very pressing question at the time. There were no fatalities, but a Stage Hand was injured.

Headlines such as 'Hippodrome Inferno' and 'Worst Fire Since The Blitz Sweeps City Centre' were emblazoned across the local press. Graphic descriptions of a huge pall of oily smoke enveloping the sky over the Centre had some foundation to them, but one reporter was thankfully letting his imagination run away with him when he wrote: 'The auditorium resembled Dante's *Inferno*. The air was filled with the vicious crackle of the lurid red flames

'Hippodrome Inferno': Denmark Street at the height of the blaze

and the crash of falling timbers. It was quickly obvious that the Hippodrome was doomed.' 'I find clusters of men soaked to the skin, their eyes red-rimmed with the smoke and fumes, plying their hoses oblivious to the danger that threatened them every minute from above,' was another piece of purple prose.

Meanwhile, back on planet Earth, the two big questions now to be faced by the owners were: would they be prepared to put up the money to rebuild and refurbish the theatre, and if so, could they get a licence to do so at a time when materials and labour for such a project remained at a premium? The council-owned Colston Hall, burned to the ground three years earlier, was still waiting for its licence to rebuild, and would not reopen until 1951. Determined to avoid any such delay, the theatre manager George Higgs met the heads of Stoll Theatres the day after the fire, and they decided to make an immediate application for a rebuilding

licence. So confident were they that it would be granted, with the weight of public opinion behind them, that they wasted little time in announcing that the opening date would be December 24 that year.

Investigators failed to establish the cause of the fire, not that their inquiries were nearly so forensically rigorous as they are today; a community that had seen half its city destroyed in the past decade was rather more fatalistic about the loss of property than it would be now. As the theatre was near-deserted at the time and the power turned off, a cigarette or match tossed away by someone going off for their lunch was accepted as the most likely cause. Doubtless one or two people who were around that day spent an anxious week or two, or maybe a good deal longer, casting their minds back and maybe searching their consciences. After all, they and a hundred of their colleagues spent the next ten months out of work or, in many cases, simply finding jobs elsewhere.

Not for the first or last time, the theatre could rely on fulsome support from the local press. West Rallies To New 'Hippo' Campaign was the banner headline in the *Bristol Evening World*, whose drama critic John Bennett's story was headlined: 'Rebuild, Says Flood Of Letters, Phone Calls.' Bennett wrote: 'There has been a swift response to the plea I made in yesterday's *Evening World* for the quick rebuilding of The Bristol Hippodrome – for a big pair of Public Scissors to cut through any red tape that might hinder the reconstruction and the re-equipment of the ruined stage.' Pressure on the local authority worked. The first consignment of steel left Scotland on September 1, the builders worked double shifts and – hey presto – *Cinderella* opened its doors on the predicted day to a public agog to view all that had been done, and very happy with what they saw, with the auditorium now resplendent in orange and gold.

A fairytale to rival *Cinderella*, then? Perhaps, but maybe not quite: it seemed mildly embarrassing, to say the least, that the show had to do battle with two other productions of the same panto in the city, at both the Empire and the Theatre Royal. Besides, in spite of tens of thou-

Bristol Evening Post: Monday 16 Feb 1948   3-Star late Edition

Rear Portion of Famous Bristol Theatre Almost Gutted

DISASTROUS BLAZE AT BRISTOL HIPPODROME

Auditorium Saved After an Hour's Battle : Warehouse Damaged

FLAMES swept through Bristol Hippodrome at lunch-time to-day in a disastrous fire which, within a few minutes, spread from the "flies" to the scenery and then enveloped the whole stage.

After an hour's battle the N.F.S. were able to announce that the auditorium had been saved—but the rear portion of the theatre was gutted, the flames leaping 30 feet into the air.

Two floors of the six-storey warehouse of Halliday's Transport, in Gaunt's Lane, were also damaged.

INTENSE HEAT CRACKS WALL

THE N.F.S. mobilised all pumps, and a turntable ladder was quickly brought into play from Denmark St., while other firemen took hoses in through the main entrance and also attempted to tackle the blaze from the stage door entrance.

A strong wind carried the flames on to Messrs. Halliday's transport warehouse and the top portion of

Great Hippodrome Fire

this also caught fire, adding to the difficulties of the firemen.

Black smoke and flames belched from top windows of Halliday's Transport.

Firemen battled with the fierce blaze on the ground floor of the Hippodrome, near one of the back exits.

Messrs. John Harvey and Sons, Ltd., wine and spirit merchants, prepared to evacuate their premises.

Crept Along Roof

The wooden timbers of the Hippodrome were an inferno and, a wall beginning to show huge cracks, it was feared it might fall.

Police cleared the streets, and volunteers assisted the N.F.S. in bringing extra lengths of hose to get more water on to the blaze.

While the flames on the Hippodrome roof had subsided to a very large extent, the fire had increased on Messrs. Halliday's warehouse and was creeping along the top floor.

When the N.F.S. arrived, flames and smoke were leaping high from the roof above the stage. Flames could also be seen leaping up at windows, and a brick wall was beginning to crack and bulge.

Awesome Scene

Inside the theatre, the spectacle was an awesome one.

Firemen were training their hoses on the burning stage from the front rows of the orchestra stalls. Burning beams were crashing on to the stage from the roof, while the fire was licking at the side boxes.

The heat inside the auditorium was intense. As far back as the refreshment kiosk behind the last row in the pit, one had to shield one's face from the heat and the glare.

As firemen ran their hoses past the box office and up the steps into the auditorium clouds of smoke poured out, driving back the hundreds of onlookers who had congregated to watch the spectacle.

Every available fireman was mobilised to fight the fire, which was located in one of the city's danger zones.

Traffic from Clifton and Park St. was diverted at College Green, while police, reinforced by colleagues, who were off duty at the time of the outbreak and men from other divisions, saw to it that onlookers kept within a safe distance of the raging inferno. Normal traffic was restored after about half-an-hour.

As I reached the Hippodrome, tele-phones an Evening Post reporter, brand new cars were being driven from the garages at the rear of the theatre to a place of safety.

A second water tower (turntable ladder) was brought into operation as the firemen endeavoured to cope with the fierce flames which were sweeping through the top floor of Halliday's warehouse.

A fireman tackling the belching flames from the top of the 60ft. tower was constantly showered with small pieces of roofing, which flew around him under the force of his jet.

Thick black smoke continued to pour from the warehouse and a pall hung over the district.

Fire Boat Used

To put on extra jets the N.F.S. brought up a fire boat to The Centre, and water was pumped up through the length of Denmark St.

By 2 p.m., when the fire had been blazing for half-an-hour, a large fissure appeared in the outer wall of the Hippodrome at the corner of Gaunt's Lane.

Among the earliest arrivals at the scene was the Deputy Lord Mayor, Ald. Gilbert S. James.

When I returned to the auditorium shortly after 2 p.m, the efforts of the firemen to prevent the fire spreading there appeared to be bearing fruit.

Although the timbers forming part of the roof over the stage had fallen in, littering the stage and wings with burning embers and scorching the front two rows of orchestra stalls, there appeared to be some hope that the blaze would be confined to that area.

The orchestra pit, covered with embers and burning fragments, was a pitiful sight. Valuable musical instruments lay in pools of water, a grand piano was burned down to the keys, and drums and other instruments were in disordered array on the ground.

Mr. Sidney Phasey, musical director, who was at home, reached the Hippodrome as firemen were removing many of the instruments from the orchestra pit.

"What a terrible tragedy this is," he said as he dashed to the place-from where, for so many years, he has conducted the Hippodrome orchestra.

Arc Lights

Powerful arc lights were carried into the Hippodrome to enable the firemen to tackle their job more effectively.

Every available piece of fire-fighting equipment was on the scene by 2 o'clock and additional firemen were reaching the narrow streets encircling the burning block as it came to the telephone.

A block of offices at the rear of Halliday's warehouse was evacuated, important documents and books being driven to the bank by employees.

Thousands of gallons of spirit in large casks were rolled from Harvey's bonded store up Orchard Lane into Orchard St. for safety.—Hundreds

Mr. S. Phasey.   Arthur Lucan.

of boxes of spirits were also carried to safety.

A band of stage hand made a daring dash into the burning building in an endeavour to save the wardrobe and properties of the performers.

Mr. Bert Jones, 69, Somerdale Av. Knowle, an assistant electrician, said they had just set the stage for the first scene for tonight's performance and left the theatre at 12.55, when everything was all right.

"We were having lunch in a near-by cafe when we saw people running up Denmark St. and following them out we saw the Hippodrome was on fire.

"The flames were coming through the grid, so, while some of us went round-the-front-and forced the front door, others went to the stage door. Inside we found the stage a mass of flames, but the dressing-rooms were intact.

continued........

Hoses Trained From Stalls

The Bristol Evening Post, 16 February 1948. The reporter described how at Harvey's bonded store in Orchard Lane, thousands of gallons of spirit in casks were rolled away to safety

sands of pounds being spent on the latest equipment, the first night did not go without a hitch. The new electronically-operated curtain refused to rise after the interval, and it was fortunate that one of the great ad-libbers, Ted Ray, had been cast as Buttons; he came out in front of the curtain and entertained the audience for some twenty minutes before the show could go on, but then again, this kind of thing was meat and drink to an old pro like him. 'Ray's a Laugh': not for nothing was that his catchphrase and besides, nobody was going to let anything spoil the big night. The outpouring of support from the Bristol public at this time of crisis underlined just how much they loved their 'Hippo'. It was a spirit that would be needed again in the dark days of the late 1970s when financial woes posed an even graver threat to the future of the theatre.

Picked out by Old Mother Riley

Arthur Lucan as Old Mother Riley

Mrs Miriam Kite of Kingswood was a teenage dancer who appeared in four Hippodrome shows in routines choreographed by Peggy Barnes from 1946-47 to 1949-50, and it was *Babes In The Wood* in 1948 that she clearly remembered best when she told her story to *The Post* at the age of eighty-one in 2012. 'The morning after the fire there was a meeting of the cast,' she recalled. 'Obviously the show was over, but Arthur Lucan chose some of us Bristol girls for his *Old Mother Riley* touring show on the Number One circuit. Jean, Margaret, Doreen, Jane, Yvonne, Hazel, Brenda, Barbara, Katy and Edith who were sisters – I still remember them all.

'Peggy Barnes was a lovely lady. We were her girls and it was through her that I started my stage career, answering her advert for dancers in 1946 and meeting her at the Theatre Royal, Bath. Some of the stars I worked with in Bristol were Ted Ray, Beryl Reid, Norman Wisdom and John Hanson in *The Desert Song*.

I toured all the Number One theatres in England and Wales but my favourite will always be The Bristol Hippodrome.' Mrs Kite told *The Post* that she still kept in trim going to Zumba and keep-fit classes – 'Oh, and I can still tap-dance!'

10

Making up for lost time

Even more than they had been after the end of the First World War, the public were hungry for light entertainment. The security old favourites brought with them was always welcome, but the mass rejection of Winston Churchill in the first post-war general election was a stark reminder that there was a new mood abroad, a pressing quest for change. One way in which this showed itself at the Hippodrome was the regular Sunday night pop concerts put on by the local impresario Charles H Lockier, not that 'pop' had quite the meaning it would go on to acquire. After all, this was still the era of big bands and light music. The first three to be booked, in April and May, 1945, highlight the cross-section of musicians who played at these concerts: Eric Winstone and his Orchestra, Leslie 'Jiver' Hutchinson and a Sunday Serenade evening with the Bristol Promenade Orchestra conducted by Sydney Phasey. As the series gained in popularity the biggest names in British dance bands started to make their way to Bristol on a Sunday evening: Ted Heath with his future pop idol vocalist Dickie Valentine, the Squadronaires, the Skyrockets, Nat Gonella and his Georgians, Carl Barriteau and his Orchestra, Felix Mendelssohn and his Hawaiian Serenaders, Maurice Winnick, Oscar Rabin, Roy Fox, Harry Roy, Jack Jackson, who would go on to become the BBC's top radio DJ.

Realising there was a following for fine singing among the Hippodrome faithful, Lockier pushed out the boat and on December 8, 1946 replaced his usual dance band offering with perhaps the world's most famous tenor, Beniamino Gigli, singing popular arias from opera along with the Neapolitan love song 'Come Back to Sorrento', which was to top the best-selling record charts for several weeks. The night was a triumph, repaying Lockier's gamble several times over. In all, he presented fifty-four pop concerts between 1945 and 1947, and it would have been one more had not the coach carrying Joe Loss and his Band broken down on the A4 at Chippenham. Joe and his boys would have been perfectly happy to make it a late night and play to as many of the audience who had waited, but the magistrates were not prepared to be so generous. The Hippodrome's Sunday licence stated that the theatre must be vacated by 8.45pm. On this point they were immovable, so much to Mr Lockier's chagrin, the audience were asked to leave and get their money back. Joe Loss, who always introduced his shows with a boisterous 'In the Mood', was a regular visitor during the war and had a large fan base, so this cancellation was particularly disappointing. But a pop concert finishing at 8.45? A curfew a year after the war had ended seems quite ludicrous to us now.

All in all, Britain was at a low ebb in the immediate post-war years, and that applied equally to the variety theatre. It was not that any other mass entertainment had taken its place, with television still unknown to almost everybody, but there was a middle-aged-to elderly feel to many of the major stars, and for young men who had seen life and death in various far-flung spots and women who had been making shells or aeroplanes and generally breaking away from the kitchen sink there was a widespread feeling that twice-nightly conjurors and jugglers and performing seals were strictly for the oldies. Rob Wilton with his endless 'The day war broke out' routine; the sand dancers Wilson, Keppel and Betty, before irony and nostalgia brought them back into focus, although far too late for them; the off-beat husband-and-wife comedy teams Nat Mills and Bobbie and Billy Caryll and Hilda Mundy: they were still heading variety bills, but to alarmingly dwindling crowds, and it was significant that when a show featuring GH Elliott, Gertie Gitana, the Bristolian Randolph Sutton and Ella Shields was assembled, it was billed as *Thanks For The Memory – August 1949*.

Occasionally, something a little different came along; Roland Petit and the Ballet Des Champs Elysees were accompanied by the London Philharmonic Orchestra, while Tom Arnold would try to shrink his highly successful Wembley Ice Revue on to the big-but-not-that-big Hippodrome stage. More bizarre by far was a show called *Hold Your Breath*, which like the ice revue arrived in 1949. It was performed mainly in an enormous tank of water, and featured an underwater striptease by Maree Leyland. By this time on-stage nudity was not uncommon; truth to tell, it was one of the tawdry and tatty gimmicks resorted to by many managements in the final desperate throes of variety, as we shall note in our review of the Fifties. But the Lord Chamberlain's rules were that the models should remain perfectly still, and the fact that Miss Leyland happened to be in a very transparent tank of water did not seem to be the strongest defence against potential obscenity charges.

Throughout this immediate post-war period manager George Higgs was to be seen regularly on the foyer stairs, cigar in hand and urging customers to 'Move along there, please'. His manner was brusque but he was much respected and admired by patrons and staff alike. Not only had he steered the ship through the dark days of war, and would then oversee the recovery from the great fire of 1948, but he would not shy away from controversy, invariably reading the public mood correctly over hot issues. For instance, he booked Gracie Fields for a week, despite the severe reservations of some. Once a queen of both stage and screen in Britain, in the early part of the war she had left for a short time to safeguard her husband, the American-Italian actor Monty Banks, who risked being interned. For this she was monstered by the press, who presented the move as little less than treason. Later she would redeem herself in most people's eyes by travelling thousands of miles entertaining the troops and raising large sums of money for service charities. Some in Bristol feared that there were still pockets of dissenters who would give her a hostile reception, but Higgs pressed ahead, and night after night she was feted by capacity houses. The only whiff of dissent centred on an arrangement of the Lord's Prayer especially written for her. Several religious groups objected to this being sung as part of a twice-nightly variety act, but she sang it with such sincerity and respect that they were left with little cause for complaint.

Later another manager, John Christie, was in the firing line when Bristol City Council decided to send a secretary to take down in shorthand every word of Max Miller's act, fearing that it was likely to pollute the minds of the audience, particularly its younger members. Perhaps they should withdraw Miller from the bill, to be sure there would be no prosecution? 'Certainly not,' Christie replied. 'There's nothing dirty about Max's act – it's all innuendo and suggestion, nudge-nudge, wink-wink. Any smuttiness is in the minds of the audience, not in what Max says. The same thing happened when I was manager of the Chiswick Empire, where a member of the watch committee sat there all week without finding a thing to complain about.' In Bristol, the guardians of public morals gave up after the second performance. A very smart operator, Max Miller.

Carroll Levis was back almost before the ink was dry on the peace treaty in his vain search for a star in Bristol – where now Cawalini and his Canine Comedians? But throughout the late Forties there was some solid theatre going on on the Hippodrome stage: Madame Louise, with *Robertson Hare*, Kenneth More in *And No Bird Sings*, Emlyn Williams in *The Winslow Boy*, a play revived to great acclaim in the West End in a radical reassessment of Terence Rattigan's work. Meanwhile, while the definition of a musical was being rewritten by Rodgers and Hammerstein across the Atlantic, the Hippodrome was still in the Ruritanian world of Ivor Novello's *Glamorous Nights*, *King's Rhapsody* and *Perchance To Dream* and Nöel Coward's *Bitter Sweet*. Still, St Augustine's Parade would get the hang of musicals in the end...

11

Stan, Ollie and the Stateside invasion

Britain was growing up in many ways, and one sign of it was the polite indifference with which we greeted some of Hollywood's biggest names when they briefly decided to try their hand in British variety; regularly for the next few years from around 1947 the London Palladium had a star from the States at the top of its bill, and many of them found their way down to the West Country. A good number of these, particularly those from the world of film, did not live up to their reputations, and their reception varied considerably. Then there came Laurel and Hardy, who certainly did not live up to expectations yet still basked in rapturous applause. By July, 1947 they were both elderly men, and robbed of the wonderful physical comedy of their long-ago films, and all the inventive props that went with them, they were reduced to a rather ordinary, stand-up routine. For once this did not matter to the 'Hippo' audience; they had come to see and pay homage to two of the greatest comic talents of the century and were determined to enjoy every moment of the experience. They roared at every well-known phrase and gesture, and their cheers as Stan and Ollie exited were tinged with a realisation that they would not see their like again. By the time they had reached Bristol in this, the first of two visits, it was well known that they had been wandering all around Britain under their own steam like lost lambs, elderly and unwell innocents abroad in a strange land where every pre-booked train ride, every new hotel, every theatre to be found was a challenge and there were still thirteen shows a week to be performed.

Mischa Auer, the 'Mad Russian' who had provided comic relief in dozens of films – his henpecked husband in the spoof Western *Destry Rides Again* is still a terrific piece of clowning – was not so generously treated by Bristol audiences. Among his supporting acts was a young Peter Sellers, and later, when he returned with his fellow Goons Harry Secombe and Spike Milligan, several people claimed they had first recognised his comic genius on the Mischa Auer bill. When Chico Marx appeared in July, 1949, few people remembered that this was not his first sighting at the theatre. Way back in 1922 he had played with his brothers Groucho, Harpo and Zeppo in a show called *Home Again*, along with future Hippodrome favourites Lucan and McShane. Like Laurel and Hardy, without the film props – and in his case, minus his priceless brothers – Chico Marx was not the comic giant he was on film; but an old hand on stage, with

62

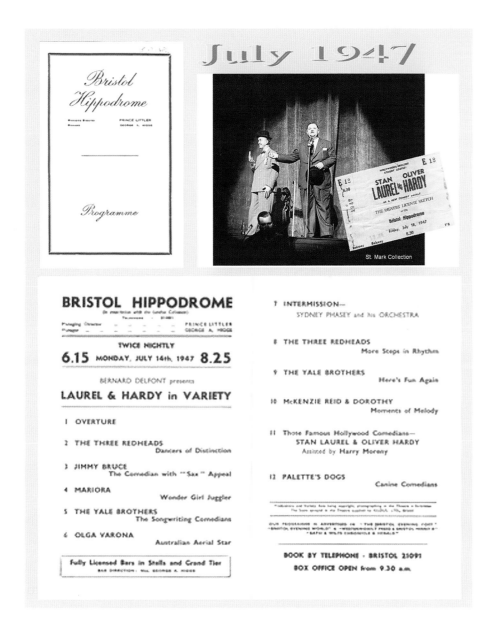

his fractured Italian and clever piano playing, at one stage even using a grapefruit to provide the harmony, he was still more than capable of entertaining an audience.

The tenor Allen Jones, who had starred with the Marx Brothers in *A Night At The Opera* and *A Day At The Races*, quickly discovered that people had a very definite reason for coming to see him – the song 'Donkey Serenade'. He had sung it to Jeannette Macdonald in *The Firefly*, and it was such a favourite in Britain that the Hippodrome crowd would not let him go until they had heard it. The song was also to haunt his son Jack, one of the most popular crooners of the 1960s. Despite a massive catalogue of hits, whenever he sang in this country he would have to give an airing of his dad's 'Donkey'.

One of Hollywood's favourite villains, the Hungarian-born Peter Lorre, was another who had started life as a stage performer. Before the rise of Hitler he had been one of the most respected character actors in Austria and Germany, and he used these skills to create an act which, while it did not bring the house down, was still well received. It was an odd show, in fact, in which, between reciting passages from Edgar Allen Poe, he gently sent-up his Hollywood image. Another mid-European, the zither-playing Anton Karas, was also an unusual but popular top-of-the-bill act. His breakthrough came when he was chosen by the director Carol Reed to compose and play the background music for Graham Greene's spy thriller *The Third Man*. Before that he had been known only among those who frequented Vienna's chain of Heuriger's wine bars, but the Harry Lime Theme changed all of that. Small with thick horn-rimmed spectacles, he looked almost forlorn as he sat in the middle of the stage, zither on his lap – but it somehow added to his evocation of a bleak, tense Vienna at the start of the Cold War.

Apart from standing on stage looking gorgeous, Jon Hall, the handsome hero of the Hollywood blockbuster *The Hurricane*, in which he romanced the sarong-clad Dorothy Lamour, did little apart from occasionally add a few notes to his wife Francis Langford's numbers; fortunately, she was one of the best big band singers of the time, and besides, the audience had the good fortune to have on the same bill one of the top ventriloquist acts on the circuit, Arthur Worsley and Charlie Brown. Television came as a godsend for Worsley, with close-ups showing the world just how good he was, but he remained a tremendous act in the halls.

Post-war Britain also welcomed a wave of African-American performers, whose visits to Europe allowed them to taste universal freedoms of the kind it would take another generation for them to achieve in their own land. Two piano-playing jazz divas, Nellie Lutcher and Rose Murphy, each went down very well, the first with her sharp diction and exaggerated pronunciation, the other full of scat buzzes and 'chee-chees' and infuriatingly infectious songs like 'Busy Line'. The Ink Spots and the Deep River Boys were vocal harmony groups who paved the way for many more in the late Fifties and Sixties, while Billy Daniels treated the Hippodrome to a string of his hits, notably 'That Old Black Magic'. Lena Horne made her entrance in 1950, took command of the stage from the off and had the audience eating out of her hand. Here was an artist with the personality to go with a voice that was equally at home singing jazz or romantic ballads.

Looking back on this Who's Who of American visitors in the forties and early fifties, it now seems incredible that one of them, Frank Sinatra, failed to sell out for any of his performances at the Hippodrome in June 1953, a couple of weeks after the coronation. He arrived in Bristol with his career at its lowest ebb, though only three months before the film *From Here to Eternity* rewrote the history book. The presence of the British bandleader Billy Ternent and his singer Eva Beynon did as much to draw in the customers as anything Frank could do, because long gone were the days of the screaming bobbysoxers, and nobody else seemed in a hurry to take their place. Then came that film, and an Oscar for best supporting actor as the doomed Private Angelo Maggio, and before he knew it his career was skyrocketing once more. Frank never again graced the 'Hippo' for a single performance, let alone a week's residency. If he had, there would not have been a seat to be found for love or money. As it was, the Sinatra Box Office receipts did not match those for the local comedians and impressionists Tony Fayne and David Evans, the French singer Jean Sablon or Max Wall, the star of that year's pantomime *Babes In The Wood*, along with Julie Andrews, still only eighteen but with a wealth of stage experience behind her. Her time to take Hollywood by storm would come.

A twice-nightly residency for Sinatra

12

Classics of their kind

In the immediate post-war period one of the most popular regular visitors to the theatre was the D'Oyly Carte Company. In those days, when Bridget D'Oyly Carte, the daughter of the original producer of Gilbert and Sullivan's comic operas, held the copyright of their work, the company would play for a fortnight, going through almost the complete run of their Savoy operas. Many enthusiasts would book a season ticket for the entire programme, and 'the gods' were always crowded by young fans who had paid seven shillings and six pence (37.5p) for their passport to see every production. A sight they always looked forward to was the entrance of the musical director, Isidore Godfrey, a spare, angular man who would insist on absolute quiet before he asked the orchestra to play the first bars of the overture. On more than one occasion a member of the audience was silenced by his withering look and even worse, his careful placing of his baton on the rostrum until the accused had fallen silent.

As far as Bristol and most provincial cities were concerned, this was a company at the height of its powers, in which first Martyn Green and then Peter Pratt delighted audiences as they quite literally followed in the footsteps of George Grossmith and Henry Lytton from Victorian times, recreating their comic business and wonderfully-delivered patter songs. Three other well loved figures, Ann Drummond-Grant as a fearsome Katisha, Fisher Morgan, the most haughty of PoohBahs, and Danell Fancourt, an imperious Mikado, delighted audiences year after year, and when Fancourt eventually stepped down, the Bristol-born, ex-Cathedral School Donald Adams took his place. Metropolitan critics scorned the D'Oyly Carte in Miss Bridget's latter days, complaining with some artistic justification that its performances had been ossified in the late nineteenth century. But oh, how the audiences loved them out on the road.

Ballet made a tentative start to becoming a regular feature at the Hippodrome, but when the Sadler's Wells Company arrived in 1943 it brought the very best in British ballet in Margot Fonteyn, Beryl Grey and Robert Helpmann. In the immediate years that followed the International Ballet Company provided good-quality fare without the aid of star names.

The Sadler's Wells Company was again responsible for grand opera gaining a foothold in Bristol. It arrived in 1944 with four operas, while Carl Rosa Opera, the company that had failed to make a great impression on its visit in 1931, found a much more responsive audience sixteen

Aida, 2007 and
Swan Lake, the Black Swan.
Both Ellen Kent Productions

years on for productions of *Rigoletto, La Bohème, Faust, La Traviata, Madama Butterfly, Il trovatore* and *Carmen*. When Sadler's Wells returned it matched Carl Rosa by presenting seven different operas and the floodgates were now open. Then there was the Bolshoi, and those with vivid recollections of the iconic Russian company's visit in August, 1963 can scarcely believe that fifty years have passed since then. Equally memorable was the queue for tickets snaking around the block within hours of the announcement that they would be coming to town. As for the domestic companies, these have changed over the years and where the theatre once had visits by the Sadler's Wells Company, English National Opera, D'Oyly Carte and Carl Rosa, now the theatre enjoys regular visits from Welsh National Opera and English National Ballet – and these branches of the arts are very much established; Sir Oswald Stoll would approve.

In drama – and for a variety house, the Hippodrome has enjoyed some worthy 'legit' moments over its hundred years – one of many highlights came in August, 1944, when a cast of some of the finest classical actors in the country assembled for *Hamlet* and *Love From Love*. John Gielgud, widely seen as the most lyrical Hamlet of his generation, was supported by Peggy Ashcroft, Leslie Banks, Miles Malleson, Yvonne Arnaud and Leon Quartermaine. The actors in these productions, presented in the grand manner, made no complaint about the size of the theatre, and neither did the audiences, who gave them a tremendous reception. But when Peggy Ashcroft returned in 1967 to play Mrs Alving in the Royal Shakespeare Company's production of Ibsen's claustrophobic *Ghosts*, there was some murmuring about the Hippodrome being the wrong venue. The critics rather agreed with this, although when interviewed later, Dame Peggy put no blame on the theatre; it was up to the director and actors to make the best of the space they were playing in, she said.

In August, 1960 the London Old Vic company visited with *Romeo And Juliet* and *The Merchant Of Venice*. Notable among the cast of the first were John Stride, Joanna Dunham, Alec McCowen and Peggy Mount – not to mention Peter Baldwin, a graduate of the West of England Theatre Company who left the Old Vic for its Bristol namesake but more famously became Mavis's chap Derek on *Coronation Street*. Stride and Dunham were again prominent in *The Merchant Of Venice*, along with Barbara Leigh-Hunt, Robert Harris, Michael Meacham and George Baker. But for star names, surely nothing will ever compare with the star-studded cast brought by the National Theatre Company for *Much Ado About Nothing* and *Hay Fever* in March, 1964. Maggie Smith, Celia Johnson, Albert Finney, Ian McKellen, Derek Jacobi, Lynn Redgrave, Robert Stephens, Michael York, Christopher Timothy, Ronald Pickup, Robert Lang... Is that enough to be going on with?

Welsh National Opera

Founded in Cardiff in 1943, Welsh National Opera first visited the Hippodrome in March, 1968 with the considerable programme of *Carmen, The Barber Of Seville, Rigoletto, Nabucco* and *Don Giovanni*. It has been returning ever since and has long been the mainstay of opera at the theatre, having appeared by the end of 2012 in one hundred and twenty productions. 'We love going there,' says Ian Douglas, the WNO Company Manager. 'It's a beautiful Matcham theatre with a long history, and it's very important to us.' There was a time when the company visited three or four times a year and even now, with its growing reputation and wider commitments worldwide, it is still in Bristol twice a year. There are many memorable performances to look back on, but Ian also has some quirky memories of the WNO in Bristol.

'I'll never forget when two Hell's Angels types walked through an open exit at the back of the stalls and made their way calmly down the centre aisle to the stage in the final act of *Tristan und Isolde*,' he recalls. 'The now Dame Anne Evans was giving it her all, and the face of Peter Rose, who was singing King Marke, was a picture.'

So is this one of those role-reversal stories, where the two stand enraptured at the front of the stalls and then toss flowers at the principals at the curtain-call?

'Not a bit of it,' says Ian. 'They stepped over the orchestra pit rail, and brushed past Sir Charles Mackerras, who was conducting, and some rather bemused violinists. Thankfully, they didn't get on the stage for their fifteen minutes of fame.'

Hell's Angels doing as Hell's Angels do at the climax of a Wagner opera. It's different, anyway.

Ian also remembers a performance of *Lucia di Lammermoor*, when half the cast and orchestra were held up on the original Severn Bridge. Sir Charles Mackerras defused the situation by giving the theatrical equivalent of an after-dinner speech, keeping everyone amused with jokes and anecdotes. He was a friend of Barry Humphries, and Dame Edna would doubtless have been proud of him that night: 'Forty-five minutes after we should have started we had most people, but not the principal tenor. Charles said: "We'll start, and if he isn't here by his first entry we'll just have to stop." He *did* get there!'

WNO *Madam Butterfly*. Cheryl Baker (Madam Butterfly).
Photo credit: Jeni Clegg

70

The Barber of Seville, 2011. L-R:
John Moore (Figaro), Eric Roberts
(Dr Bartolo), Laura Parfitt (Rosina),
and Colin Lee (Count Almaviva).
Photo credit: Johan Persson

Others in Bristol swear that the WNO holds the record for being the only company to receive cheers and applause when announcing that a leading singer would have to be replaced at the last moment. It was in March, 2006, when a capacity house was settling itself to enjoy a much-praised production of Wagner's *The Flying Dutchman* that the announcement came over that the leading man had been struck down with a throat infection and would be replaced; an audible sigh of frustration immediately turned to loud cheering when the substitute turned out to be one Bryn Terfel.

Ellen Kent

Finally, for the first ten years of the new millennium it was left to the dynamic 'pocket battleship' of an independent producer, Ellen Kent, to supply most of the other operatic offerings, plus a little ballet. Bursting with energy and enthusiasm from her five-foot-nothing frame, she brought many Eastern European companies to the Hippodrome, and as their originally rather formal and static presentations adapted to Western tastes and grew in stature, so the Bristol audiences took them to their hearts as the years passed by.

13

Playing for the love of it

The thought of appearing on the Hippodrome stage has enthralled generations of young performers in this part of the world, and those who have appeared there will forever remember the experience. It is a tradition that goes back a long way. In the First World War several local singing and dancing groups emerged, usually in shows raising funds for good causes – the Bristol Glee Singers in a Grand Fashionable Matinee for the Lord Mayor's Hospital Fund in 1915, the Royal Orpheus Glee Society and Cecilian Choral Society and then dancers from the Misses Parnall School in concerts for the Serbian Red Cross, Scottish women's hospitals and the Actors' Church Union, the charity that issued travelling theatre people with their lists of digs. Ten years later the Misses Parnall were still supporting charity events, this time in aid of the Church of England Waifs and Strays' home at Wick House, Brislington. That charity still exists as the Children's Society.

In 1924 Kathleen Maddock's dancing school appeared on the programme, and for decades her girls graced the Hippodrome stage before a local producer and director, Jimmie Morris, spotted an opening and went for it with his Bristol Musical Comedy Club (BMCC). In the 1950s it was still difficult to tour a big company, so apart from troupes headed by the likes of John Hanson, who was the Red Shadow for at least two decades in his production of *The Desert Song,* few West End shows found themselves immediately bound for the provinces after their London runs. Morris's society eased itself in in 1955 with the pre-war light opera *Wild Violets,* with music by the *White Horse Inn* composer Robert Stoltz, but twelve months later it was back with a bang with a lively *Oklahoma!* It was an enormous success, and the start of the club's long and happy relationship with the theatre. Over the years, local talent was showcased in such offerings as *Carousel, Annie Get Your Gun, South Pacific, Guys And Dolls* and *My Fair Lady,* while *Camelot,* with original costumes from Drury Lane, was a visual treat. Not all the club's ventures were winners, however, and *How To Succeed In Business Without Really Trying,* with music and lyrics by the *Guys And Dolls* supremo Frank Loesser, proved too American for local audiences.

A second local society, the Bristol Light Opera Club (BLOC), followed the BMCC into the theatre with *The Gypsy Baron* in 1956 and more than half a century later it still feels at home

Bristol Light Opera Club's production of *Beauty And The Beast*

here, having brought the non-professional UK premieres of *Evita, The Witches Of Eastwick* and *Beauty And The Beast* to the Hippodrome stage. When BLOC celebrated its fiftieth anniversary in 1983 with *The Great Waltz* it had a royal visitor in Princess Anne. Members had been told she would be leaving shortly after the show, but far from it, she surprised and delighted them by staying on for the on-stage party. In April the previous year Princess Margaret had led a glittering array of guests at the theatre for a gala performance by the Sadler's Wells Royal Ballet in aid of Wells Cathedral.

On two occasions, in 1972 during their first production of *Fiddler on the Roof*, and 2000, when they presented *Scrooge*, members of BLOC took to the air over the stage, with mixed results. Merion Ashton who was to become a BLOC stalwart, was cast as the ghost of Lazar Wolf's late wife Fruma Sarah in the 1972 production, and each night, in the flying harness used by Margaret Lockwood and Sarah Churchill in *Peter Pan*, she would stand on a twenty-foot-high platform in the wings awaiting her cue. At the dress rehearsal the Stage Manager,

April 1982: a visit from HRH Princess Margaret for a gala evening in aid of Wells Cathedral

Jack Marriott, solemnly informed Merion that she was not to jump off her perch until he had checked that all the weighted balances were in place, after which he would give her the signal. Merion, her Welsh accent accentuated by sheer terror, replied that if he didn't give her a push, she would still be up there come Christmas. Despite all the precautions, however, one evening, instead of sailing upwards and out over the audience, she plunged straight down towards the stage and hit it with her thigh before soaring up and away in the right direction. At this point, as the ghost, she was supposed to let out a blood-curdling scream, but it came early that night, when she hit the stage. Good trouper as she was, she was back the next night, her badly bruised leg heavily strapped beneath her flowing costume. Then again, it was decided that Robert Hurst, playing the title role in the 2000 production of *Scrooge*, did not require such an elaborate harness as Merion, as his progress had only to be upward and around the stage area, rather than out over the audience. All went well during the dress rehearsal and for the first couple of performances, but then, as he took to the air, instead of staying facing the audience he suddenly began to revolve gently in a way that did not go with the quite serious song he was singing. Unintentionally, he brought the house down.

BLOC Productions provided much of the cast to celebrate the theatre's seventy-fifth anniversary, and, as we have noted, the current centenary. The 1987 show had started with the scene from *The Sands o' Dee* where the hero rescues Mary, and although the water tank had long been dismantled, a very nervous tenor, Roland Kitchen, entered from stage left riding a white steed. All went well until it was time to exit stage right, when the horse decided it did not know what was awaiting it out there in the blackness and eventually turned around to face the way it had come on. It carried the hero and heroine off in fine style – on its own terms.

A lifetime of shows from BLOC Productions

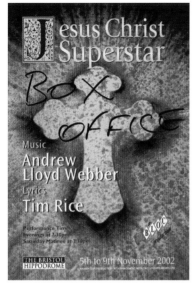

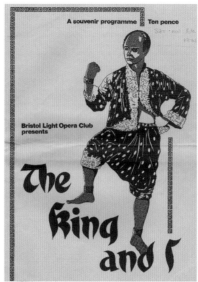

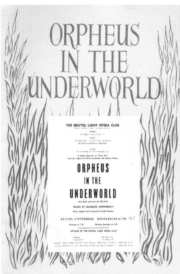

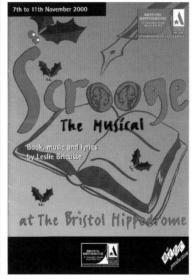

Yesterday's Island

Another original show written, composed and presented by a local group at the Hippodrome was *Yesterday's Island*, a musical comedy based on the life and times of inner-city St Philips Marsh from 1926 to 1956. It was in fact the third presentation of this account of a self-contained part of Bristol which in the period covered had a population of around six thousand people, and it was on the back of profits from the second production that the third was mounted at the Hippodrome – and then the fourth. With social changes and rehousing the old 'Island' community had disappeared, but there were still many people around for whom the events dramatised were within living memory and they, their families and friends ensured that there was no shortage of customers waiting to relive this part of comparatively recent Bristol history as written and produced by John Scully, narrated by Steve Long and promoted by Brian Davies.

'The story goes back to 1983, when there was a St Philips Marsh reunion and it was decided between four of us that we should publish a book on the district where we were all born and grew up,' says Roger Packer, now of Hanham. 'Four thousand copies of *Yesterday's Island* were printed and sold out, and while the interest was unbelievable, I honestly thought that was the end of matter. Then two local people, Brian Davies and John Scully, decided to take it to this next stage. A cast of seventy was involved and in 1986 the show was taken to the Hippodrome, where it was watched by packed audiences. I don't think that anyone could believe that something taken from a small book and performed by amateurs could be such a success.

'There was such demand that the show was again staged in 1987, again to sell-out crowds and standing ovations. In the end, when totalled up, we realised that fifty thousand people had seen *Yesterday's Island*. I believe the critics were right when they called it "the best amateur show ever staged at The Bristol Hippodrome". I know that many people who saw it could relate to it; so many said "It was like that where I lived". I feel very proud that my late wife and I were involved, and that a group of us got together and made it to The Bristol Hippodrome. My only regret is that this show should not have ended in 1987. In the West End, staged with professional actors, I know it would have been a smash hit. *Yesterday's Island* could relate to anywhere in Britain. It was a lot of hard work, but what wonderful memories of The Bristol Hippodrome.'

Another venture that cemented the relationship between the Hippodrome and the local community for many years was the Scouts' *Gang Show*. It had long been the ambition of Scout-masters Eric Foxley and Graham Franklin, both of whom had long associations with the Western Opera Players and Bristol Musical Comedy Club, to produce such a show, and after testing the strength of support for it in smaller venues, it arrived at the Hippodrome in 1972 and stayed there for the next thirty-six years. Crewkerne-born Ralph Reader, who first dreamed up the gang show idea in 1932, was a frequent visitor, and indeed had written many of the sketches. 'Crest of a Wave', a song he had composed for the first London production, always featured prominently, and indeed was by this time the signature tune of gang shows throughout the world. It had first been heard at the Hippodrome in 1952, in Reader's touring show *Meet the Gang*.

Although non-professional Bristol performers have appeared individually and in the casts of professional shows throughout the theatre's history it is rare that an original show written, composed and presented by a local group takes over the Hippodrome, but a notable exception was an original opera, *Clifton Town*, in 1977. Written and composed by civil engineer and opera buff John Humphries, it was the story of the Bristol Riots of 1831; the topic had always fascinated John, and his experience of appearing at the Hippodrome with Bristol Light Opera prompted him to try to stage it there. He finally found a slot sandwiched between a Billy Connolly extravaganza and a children's show, *Rupert And The Outlaws*. John and a company made up of BLOC and Bristol Opera members won many friends with this take on a key moment in local history; but despite good grassroots support, with few sponsors and no public money behind them, they found themselves paying for the privilege of playing the Hippodrome.

14

A time of change

The Fifties and early Sixties were changing times in Britain and changing times at the Hippodrome. The death of variety had been predicted from the onslaught of talking pictures in the late Twenties, but on the Number One circuit, at least, there was still money to be made from it. In fact, while television would eventually toll its death knell, at the big venues it was at first by no means a complete disaster. See Benny Hill or Norman Wisdom in the corner of your sitting room on the glamorous new medium one week and then catch them in real life, for longer, in your home town the next: that sounded pretty good to a lot of people.

The key words, of course, were Number One circuit. By this stage, lesser theatres had resorted to the tawdry titillation in an attempt to pull in some kind of crowd, as often as not lone men in long mackintoshes. Stock-still nudes and thrusting dancing girls wearing not very much but enough to beat the censor: variety was no longer family or even mixed-sex entertainment at the lower end of the scale. At Old Market, the Empire, for so long a thorn in the Hippodrome's flesh, succumbed to the inevitable and closed in 1954 – but not before its owner, the colourful Freddie Butterworth, had mounted a stout defence of an artistic policy in which Peaches Page, The Star Without A Bra, was seen as one of his classier acts.

The old pro Wee Georgie Wood had used his column in the trade paper *The Stage* to take up the cudgels on behalf of a reader from Northampton who had complained about the fare on offer at Butterworth's theatre in Northampton. 'Figures and facts prove beyond all measure of doubt that the clean, first-class entertainment presented in Northampton for the last three years has proved a financial loss,' Freddie replied. 'The so-called cheap nude shows have shown a financial gain, unfortunately – and I say "unfortunately" because I would be one of the first to rejoice if the public supported clean entertainment, but then, what can we expect? Is it not a fact that the national newspapers with the largest circulations are the ones which deal in dirt and sex? Is it not a fact that on all the book stalls, ninety-five per cent of the magazines exhibited are exploiting sex? Are not the most popular and successful films today those with an X certificate? Why should the stage take all the blame? We are just one of the "small runners" trying to keep up with the public's lowering taste. Of course, if we wish to attempt to re-educate the public, I am all for it: with a £2,500,000 grant subsidy from the Chancellor of the

Sean Connery

Sean Connery joined the chorus of the Theatre Royal, Drury Lane production of *South Pacific* in June, 1953, but by the time it reached the Hippodrome in November that year he had graduated to a small talking part as Marine Corporal Hamilton Steeves. At the same time he was understudying two juvenile lead parts, and his wages had risen from £12 to £14 10s. Since he had gone into acting merely by chance and had been in it for less than six months when he reached Bristol, it is clear that he was not slow to make his mark. He had visited London from Edinburgh to take part in a Mr Universe contest at the Scala Theatre, where he came third in the tall men's class. One of the other boys there told him that they were auditioning for the chorus of *South Pacific*, and he was on his way...

Exchequer I would start the campaign tomorrow.'

Wee Georgie, somewhat disingenuously, retorted that Peter Brough, Max Bygraves, Ted Ray 'and a host of others' managed to pack theatres and cinemas, demonstrating that the public would support clean entertainment. To which Freddie Butterworth might well have replied: 'Brough, Bygraves, Ray? If only...' But the Hippodrome could and did afford such names, and indeed 'a host of others'. In 1954, the year in which the Empire went under, variety at St Augustine's Parade boasted a Who's Who of British light entertainment at or near the top of the bill: Max Bygraves, Vic Oliver, Bob and Alf Pearson, Norman Evans, Dickie Valentine, Josef Locke, Harry Worth, Pearl Carr and Teddy Johnson, Billy Cotton, Wilfred Pickles, the Beverley Sisters, Max Miller, Arthur English, Jewel and Warriss, Hylda Baker, plus the Americans Al Martino and Guy Mitchell. Then again, you had to go to the Sadler's Wells productions if you wanted to see Margot Fonteyn.

By 1960, however, even the Hippodrome was struggling to put on more than half a dozen variety shows a year, with some of those no longer starring old-stagers from the halls but the

FORTHCOMING ATTRACTIONS

MARCH 28th	ONE WEEK

Britain's Exciting New
Recording Star

ADAM FAITH

Top Disc Seller of
"WHAT DO YOU WANT"
and "POOR ME"

★

APRIL 4th	ONE WEEK

We invite you to relax and listen to the
voice of...

MICHAEL HOLLIDAY

AND USUAL BIG
VARIETY BILL

APRIL 11th	ONE WEEK

LARRY PARNES presents
TWO SENSATIONAL
AMERICAN DISC STARS

Gene Vincent
and
Eddie Cochran

A TERRIFIC "BIG BEAT"
SUPPORTING COMPANY

APRIL 18th	ONE WEEK

TV's Fastest Spectacular

**Black and White
Minstrel
Show**

TERRIFIC CAST OF TV STARS
Produced by GEORGE INNS

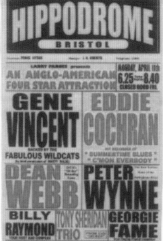

Eddie Cochran

Paul McCartney and Wings departing after their 1973 show

new breed of pop idols who had been catapulted to stardom on the strength of a couple of hit records. Their limitations were all too cruelly exposed when they topped the bill on *Sunday Night at the London Palladium* on TV, but live and with the girls in the audience screaming, they could just about get away with it. Adam Faith and Anthony Newley, the latter of whom really did have stagecraft, headed two such shows, with tight, savvy bands behind them in the John Barry Seven and Don Lang and his Frantic Five. Out-and-out pop show tours were still rare at this venue – after all, everyone knows that The Beatles, Stones and Cliff Richard never played the Hippodrome, and the fact that Paul McCartney did so later with Wings is generally seen as no consolation at all. A genuine all-music show came in May, 1961, a *Rock and Trad Spectacular* with Billy Fury, Joe Brown, Georgie Fame, Mark Wynter and Vince Eager; not much Trad there. But the booking that truly hit the headlines, and is still a landmark in rock history to this day, was the quaintly titled *A Fast-Moving Anglo-American Beat Show*.

Top of the bill were Gene Vincent and the Wildcats, and Georgie Fame and Johnny Gentle were also doing their thing. Second on the bill was an American kid who had made modest in-roads into the charts in this country, with one Top Ten hit, one in the Top Twenty and two in the Top Thirty. Up until April 16, 1960, only the hippest kids in school knew much about Eddie Cochran. By April 17 he was all over every evening paper in the country. His week at Bristol had been marred by illness – he had worn dark glasses and apologised for a sore throat – but for him the up-side was that after the Saturday night Hippodrome show he and his song-writer girlfriend Sharon Sheeley would be hopping into a taxi and hightailing it to Heathrow for an overnight flight back to the States after a long and gruelling tour. The show ran late, and people milling around Denmark Street were alarmed by the speed at which a two-tone Cortina was nosing along towards St Augustine's Parade, where a left turn would have it on the A4 in no time. As the world was soon to learn, its journey ended just outside Chippenham, when it left the road and Cochran, only twenty-one, suffered injuries from which he died a few hours later. Also in the car and injured was Gene Vincent, a gnarled old rocker – or so he seemed to teenagers – whose distinguishing feature was a pronounced limp which everyone presumed, rightly or wrongly, was the result of another road accident, on a motorbike. Why was beautiful Eddie, a James Dean lookalike with a similar rebellious persona, the one who had to die? Today, a stone marks the site of the tragedy – and at The Bristol Hippodrome, where towering stars by the thousand have kept audiences captivated for a century, the only one to be commemorated by a plaque in the foyer is Eddie Cochran.

15

The tough trail to prosperity

Out of fashion and out of luck, two British musicals that previewed in the early 1960s at the Hippodrome met with only modest success when they transferred to London. Despite its leading lady Elaine Stritch winning rave notices and the composer Nöel Coward attracting yards of publicity when he arrived in Bristol by helicopter to view a performance, audience response was only lukewarm to the musical *Sail Away* in 1962. Although several of his plays were successfully presented at the Hippodrome – including that visit by Margaret Lockwood as Amanda in *Private Lives* – the theatre was not a happy hunting ground for the Master's musicals. His first sight of his *After The Ball*, based on Oscar Wilde's *Lady Windermere's Fan*, came on April 1, 1955, and like the rest of the audience, he was not impressed. He said he had been prepared for the fact that the theatre was so enormous that it would dwarf the production, but not for 'restless, untidy direction' which led to 'everyone moving about so much during the dialogue scenes and the numbers, leaving a great deal of the performance inaudible'. He and his confidante, the actress Joyce Carey, were equally underwhelmed by his leading ladies, the former Ivor Novello favourites Mary Ellis and Vanessa Lee. The first, he said, sang poorly, and the second's acting was below par. There was predictable praise for Irene Browne, a long-time Coward favourite, and Graham Payn, who just happened to be his life partner, but as he informed the director, the distinguished choreographer Robert Helpmann, 'in its present state, if it opened in London it would not last a week'. In fact when it did finally reached the West End, Bristol's verdict was fully justified and it struggled to last for 188 performances.

Sail Away and *After the Ball* might have been mild disappointments for Coward and his many fans, but their fate was happier than the one that awaited the sumptuously staged *Vanity Fair*, which arrived in 1963. Its music was by Julian Slade, whose *Salad Days*, which had started life close by at the Theatre Royal, was about to break the record for the longest-running musical in the West End. As for the cast, *Vanity Fair* starred Dame Sybil Thorndike, George Baker, Michael Aldridge and Frances Cuka, fresh from her triumph as Jo in Shelagh Delaney's *A Taste Of Honey* in London and New York. It looked like a sure-fire winner, but it decidedly was not, and this was also the fate of the much-vaunted Leonard Bernstein musical setting of Voltaire's novella *Candide* after it had opened in April 1959. It was savaged by the local critics, as it would later be by the national press. The leading man, Denis Quilley, escaped unscathed, but not the female lead, the American Mary Costa. Already well established in opera and operetta, she had recently received tremendous praise for her voicing of Princess Aurora in the newly released Disney cartoon *Sleeping Beauty*. Leonard Bernstein was an enorrnous fan and he leapt to her defence, accusing the critics of not knowing their jobs. But all his blusterings failed to change the Bristol and later London public's opinion of *Candide*, and it was consigned to the long litany of expensive failures.

And this was the problem – a major problem. The Hippodrome had been struggling financially for years by the early sixties and into the seventies, and it desperately needed a change of fortune, with variety now consigned completely to history and nothing apparently on the horizon to take its place. So often a production would seem to be full of promise and potential profit, and then it would die quite spectacularly. It happened again in 1975 with *Jeeves*. The first preview shows threatened to run into the early hours of the morning, and despite endless rewrites of Alan Ayckbourn's script and drastic cuts to Andrew Lloyd Webber's score, there was nothing David Hemmings as Wooster and the rest of the cast could do to rescue it. It went on to last just thirty-eight performances in the West End, and though it fared slightly better in a 1996 revival, it is now remembered as Lloyd Webber's only real flop. More to the point as far as the Hippodrome was concerned, its failure could not have come at a worse time. In February, 1975 the Musicians' Union named the Hippodrome as one of a dozen provincial theatres it would boycott unless backstage facilities were greatly improved, a threat backed by English National Opera, which cut its two-week visit to one.

Bryan Matheson, who had two spells at the theatre as manager and also knew it as an actor in *The Desert Song* and Coward's *Bitter Sweet*, was quick to rush to the Hippodrome's defence. 'I've been all over the country as a performer and I've worked from dressing rooms that would make this place look like a palace,' he said. 'Many people have come to me and said "You must keep this theatre open".' Unfortunately, the only funds on offer for any renovation were £40,000 from the Arts Council, and with no hope of the city council, individuals or local businesses raising the remainder of the £140,000 urgently needed for the facelift, the future looked almost as bleak as it had after the fire of 1948.

The once all-powerful group that owned the theatre had just four venues left by 1977, and its Managing Director Louis Benjamin admitted that The Hippodrome was under 'severe surveillance'. 'Stage Set For Quiet Farewell', the local press concluded, and when the long-

1979: Dame Anna Neagle in *My Fair Lady*

serving Stage Director Jack Marriott and Chief Electrician Derek Peel retired, they admitted that they feared that the theatre might be going with them. Rumoured potential buyers included Associated Television, while also in the frame were a charitable trust formed by local businessmen and a surprise bidder, Avon County Council, which offered £150,000 for the freehold plus a small percentage of the theatre's revenue. Equity, the actors' trade union, petitioned the Prime Minister James Callaghan to intervene in the fate of this and six other provincial theatres, and organised a picket outside the Hippodrome led by members of the cast of the current show, *Rupert And The Outlaws*.

Marjorie Bleasdale, who headed a Save Our Hippodrome campaign which daily gathered momentum and supporters, once again showed the theatre owners and local authorities just what this theatre meant to the people of Bristol and its surrounding areas. She and her colleagues worked hard to collect more than two thousand signatures, while once again the local press rallied to the cause; indeed, it had been doing so for the past decade or more, for as early as June, 1963 Peter Rodford was ringing alarm bells in the *Western Daily Press*. In an interview with the then Manager, John Christie, he wrote: 'Earlier this week, while the London Ballet was dancing *Les Sylphides* and *The Nutcracker*, I celebrated with John Christie... his forty years in theatre management with a drink in the Stalls Bar. The conversation was convivial and carefree, but he must have wished he could have reached this milestone in happier circumstances. Less than a fortnight before, he had the unpleasant duty of laying off many of the staff – and tomorrow night he will see the curtain fall, not to rise again for another ten weeks. The news of the long summer closure had arrived in the post from head office on the day he returned from holiday.'

Financial problems were to dog the theatre for the next fifteen years, until they reached crisis point in 1978. All the hard work Marjorie Bleasdale and her team put in at that time, and the goodwill of the local authority and press, could not prevent the announcement – after a Jasper Carrott concert, to add an air of absurdity to the proceedings – that forty staff would be given their notice in May, and no more shows would be booked after June 3. The outlook could not have been bleaker than it had been during the dark days of the Blitz – but then, from out of the blue, came a life-saving twist as improbable as anything ever seen on stage. In brief, Stoll did a U-turn and changed their minds. The Hippodrome would not be allowed to fail. The reason why has never been fully explained. Prince Littler, its owner since 1942, had always said this was his favourite provincial theatre and had vowed never to close it – but he had been dead since 1973 and since then the chairmanship of Stoll-Moss Theatres had been in the hands of Associated Television's larger-than-life Sir Lew Grade. Maybe, just maybe, this media heavyweight still harboured happy memories of his days as world charleston champion, when he had performed at the Hippodrome twice in the 1930s alongside such luminaries as Randolph Sutton and Hamilton Conrad's pigeons. Then again, perhaps the *volte-face* was something to do with the full or near-full houses the theatre was suddenly pulling in with recent shows, not least the John Inman pantomime *Mother Goose*. Whatever the reason, The Bristol Hippodrome was the one the management chose to retain, while selling off the remainder of their provincial theatres.

It was in 1984, six years later and in a rapidly changing and more transient and international leisure industry, that the Hippodrome finally passed out of the ownership of the company that carried (in some form) the name of its original head, Sir Oswald Stoll. In truth by this time the link was tenuous. As we have noted, the showman Prince Littler had acquired the Stoll theatres on Sir Oswald's death in 1942, and by 1947 he had also become chairman of the (once again) rival Moss Empires chain, reuniting the two to create Stoll-Moss Theatres in 1960. By 1984 Lew Grade had been replaced as chairman by Robert Holmes a'Court – a buccaneering Australian 'corporate raider' who had already snapped up ATV's parent company, Associated Communications Corporation. At the same time, Holmes a'Court bought Stoll-Moss Theatres' London houses, which in 2000 were acquired by Sir Andrew Lloyd Webber; with eleven West End theatres, including the Palladium, (the group ensures that the Stoll legacy lives on, if not in Bristol). The buyer of the Hippodrome, reportedly for just under a million pounds, was Apollo Leisure, which in a very short period of time had been built up by the ambitious young impresario Paul Gregg into Britain's largest theatre group.

On paper, the ownership of the Hippodrome from 1984 to 2009, when it passed into the hands of the Ambassador Theatre Group (ATG), looks bewildering: 1999, SFX; 2000, Clear Channel Entertainment; 2005, Live Nation. The changes must certainly have kept the staff on their toes, but all came not through sales of groups of theatres by parent companies but the sale, merger or reorganisation of the parent companies themselves. In 1999, Gregg sold Apollo Leisure, which included twenty-three venues and the sales company Tickets Direct, for £158 million to the American conglomerate SFX; a year later, SFX were bought for 4.4 billion dollars and merged with another Stateside giant, Clear Channel Entertainment; and in 2005, Live Nation emerged as an off-shoot of Clear Channel. Not a straightforward progression, certainly, but maybe one not quite so piecemeal and random as the bald list of changes of ownership might suggest.

It was in June, 2009 that Live Nation, with arena promotions and a merger with Ticketmaster now its priorities, put its entire stock of seventeen British venues on the market with a price tag of £75 million. At first some twenty parties expressed interest, but the field was soon narrowed down to three, with Ambassador Theatre Group, then the UK's second-largest theatre owner/operator eventually triumphant. The final figure was reported to be £90 million, and the company co-founded by Sir Howard Panter and Rosemary Squire OBE in 1992 was now the biggest theatre operator in the country, with thirty-nine venues (rising to 40 with the acquisition of The Foxwoods Theatre on Broadway in 2013). 'Our aim is to help maintain the shows and theatres as vibrant successes,' said Sir Howard Panter. 'This is the start of a very exciting chapter for everyone, as we move forward together to deliver quality entertainment and outstanding customer service across the UK,' was Rosemary Squire's verdict. So it has proved.

16

Never-to-be-forgotten

We have already noted the record-breaking success of Disney's *The Lion King* in the Hippodrome's centenary season, but there have been so many memorable moments over the years. Here, in chronological order are ten of the best – but the top ten? That's for every reader to decide for themselves.

1953, Guys and Dolls

It was not until *Guys and Dolls* burst on the scene in May, 1953 that the practice of trying out shows before they hit the West End became part of the Hippodrome's profile. It came crammed with the stars – Vivian Blaine, Sam Levene, Jerry Wayne and the then lesser-known Stubby Kaye – who had made the show the biggest hit for years on Broadway. Better still, there was the addition of a popular West End star as the mission girl Sarah Brown – the vivacious Lizbeth Webb, who was already popular in the city through her performance as Lucy Veracity Willow in *Bless the Bride*. A packed opening night audience gave this musical version of Damon Runyon stories an enthusiastic thumbs-up, and they cheered for encore after encore when Stubby Kaye as Nicely-Nicely Johnson sang an intricately choreographed 'Sit Down You're Rocking the Boat'. Kaye was the least known Broadway import on opening night, and the best known and loved by the time the show finished its run.

1960-61, Aladdin

A huge name in British films from the mid-1930s, George Formby had found himself out of fashion with movie fans after the Second World War but was still a big draw in variety, with his cheeky grin, saucy songs and quite brilliant banjolele playing. His bill-topping father appeared at the Hippodrome during and shortly after the First World War and young George quickly forsook his ambitions to be a jockey and decided to follow in his footsteps after his death in 1921. It was when he made his first appearance in a book musical that he fully re-established himself with theatre audiences. After the Second World War it was his performance as the gullible Percy Piggott in *Zip Goes A Million* that won him a new host of fans, but six months into the show's London run he suffered a heart attack and was not fit when the tour took it to Bristol. Now, a decade on, in *Aladdin*, with Vanessa Lee, Valentine Dyall and Edmund Hockridge, he was at last able to treat Hippodrome audiences to all his famous songs, from 'Leaning on a Lamp-post' to 'Oh Mr Wu', 'When I'm Cleaning Windows' and 'With My Little Stick of Blackpool Rock'. (What Blackpool rock had to do with Old Peking is a question only panto fans can answer.) Unhappily, he had to end the show early because of a recurrence of his heart problems, and he died in hospital in Preston a month after *Aladdin* closed.

1961, The Music Man

This preview of a top American show brought the MGM star Van Johnson to Bristol and subsequently London. He was somewhat hurt by his performance as the loveable con man 'Professor' Harold Hill being unfavourably compared with that of the original Broadway star Robert Preston, but he had happy memories of his stay in Bristol, particularly his regular after-show suppers in Marco's restaurant. By no means as laid-back and happy-go-lucky as his amiable image suggested, he was particularly fond of fried chicken followed by banana fritter and had been told that Marco's, on the steps off Baldwin Street to St Nicholas Market, did the best in town. Unfortunately, on his first visit there the chef had gone home for the night – it was, after all, after 10pm! – but his pleas fell on receptive ears. The widow who came in late each night to clear up said she knew exactly how the chef did chicken and bananas, Johnson took up her offer and was so impressed that he returned many times, always insisting that she should do the cooking. He also gave her and her young son tickets for the show, and for many years sent them Christmas cards. Also in the cast was the twelve-year-old Dennis Waterman, and his performance as the shy, lisping Winthrop Paroo making a desperate attempt to sing Gary Indiana without spluttering too badly won him many fans. Culinary footnote: maybe readers who wish to live to ninety-two, as Van Johnson did, should build their diet around fried chicken and banana fritters. Maybe.

1975, Joseph And the Amazing Technicolor Dreamcoat

Hot on the heels of his expensive flop *Jeeves*, in April, 1975 Andrew Lloyd Webber was back with the tried-and-tested *Joseph*, created with his original collaborator, Tim Rice. It was to be Bristol's first viewing of a musical that would attract its own cult following and return at regular intervals for the best part of the next forty years, and Phillip Schofield was the high profile star to play the title role. On one of these visits the company earned the respect of the audience for continuing in the face of adversity, for in a near-replay of the first night of *Cinderella* after

the great fire of 1948, the safety curtain refused to rise. This time, however, there was no Ted Ray on hand to entertain the audience while the problem – a broken chain – was fixed. It emerged that the only place to find a replacement was Halford's, but of course the shop was closed and an appeal to the audience for anyone who worked there fell on deaf ears. It ended up with the second half performed in front of the 'iron' in a concert version. A few in the audience walked out but most did not, appreciative of the efforts of Phillip Schofield and the rest of the cast and stage crew to ensure that the show went on.

1976, The Black and White Minstrel Show

A break from the traditional panto came in 1976 with a visit from the then most popular light entertainment show on British television. It was a move that paid off handsomely, with record bookings. The Minstrels, developed by George Mitchell from his George Mitchell Glee Club, hold a unique place in the history of British theatre. For twenty years, from 1958 to 1978, they regularly drew weekly audiences of eighteen million on TV; their stage show occupied London's Victoria Palace for 6,477 performances; and when they came on tour, choosing the Hippo-

Eartha Kitt

Eartha Kitt's peak was in the Fifties, as the sexy, feline singer of suggestive songs that beat the censor only because of the knowing, self-parodying style in which she presented them. But she continued to wow audiences up until shortly before her death through cancer in 2008, and two men in Bristol still remember with affection her one and only show at the Hippodrome in March, 1990.

One of them is Stage Door Keeper Tony Bell. 'In those days I had to wear a green jacket with gold braid and buttons,' he says. 'They decided that at a certain point of the show Eartha would be served champagne, and asked if I would do it. I don't like the thought of being on stage, but I reluctantly said I would, for a consideration. What they didn't tell me was that the champagne would be going down my neck, rather than hers. I polished off the bottle in about twenty minutes, after which I had to get back into the wings in one piece. Even without the drink I reckon I'd done enough for my Equity card. Then all I had to do was finish my shift at the Stage Door...

'One of the guys in the band said whatever you do, don't look at her. Look into her eyes, and you'll completely lose the plot. So I concentrated on the people in the front row, and got through that way. Afterwards she came up and thanked me for doing it, but I was a bit tipsy by then and couldn't come up with anything more memorable than: "Thasha pleashure..."'

The other man with treasured memories of that night is the distinguished Bristol artist Trevor Haddrell, who was a fan of hers for more than fifty years. 'The first time we met was when I was seventeen and journeyed to London to see her perform in cabaret there,' he recalls. 'I'd taken along a life-sized painting I'd done of her and intended to leave it at the Box Office – but to my amazement I found myself being ushered to her dressing room by her manager to present it to her in person. She laughed at my trembling hands as I held it up for her to see. "Come here and sit beside me," she said. "I'm only flesh and blood like you, you know!"'

The two kept in touch via regular letters after that, and Trevor saw her shows whenever he could. His last contact with her came when she phoned him out of the blue not long before she died. 'She told me I'd always been very special to her,' he says, clearly still moved, but his day of days will forever be that Hippodrome visit. 'I went straight from a busy day teaching at Clifton High to meet her in her suite at the Unicorn Hotel,' he says. 'After a while she called her limousine and came with me to see my "cute little cottage" in Clifton Wood. Later my partner had a brass plaque put on the wall to commemorate the event! She gave a knock-out performance that night, as she always did, and directed one song straight at me in the front row – 'I Can't Give You Anything But Love, Baby'. I melted in my seat. Afterwards she said she wanted to eat fresh pasta, and I took her to Trattoria da Renato on King Street, where she was treated like royalty – and loved the pasta. It's been hard not to view my life since that day as a bit of an anti-climax!'

drome as their first venue in 1960, Bristol was far from alone in breaking Box Office records. Of course they were not the first black-face entertainers to visit. Eugene Stratton did that when he topped the bill on the opening night in 1912, and GH Elliott was a regular visitor from the early days to the 1950s. Al Jolson, the most famous of them all, never came to Bristol, but his brother Harry did, in 1930. Developed in America in the first half of the 1900s, minstrel shows were at the height of their popularity around the end of that century and the beginning of the next. Even during the Black and White Minstrels' twenty-year heyday they were seen by the majority as non-controversial, middle-of-the-road family entertainers; but attitudes changed radically after that, and when the show returned to multi-cultural Bristol in 1992 the uproar was such that it was agreed that the artists would not wear black make-up, apart from a brief Al Jolson impersonation. And though the package was rebranded *That Old Minstrel Magic*, that was the end of minstrel shows.

1993, Cats

Those haunting cat's eyes peered down over Bristol from posters for almost all of 1993, for this was the show that notched up the equal record run at the Hippodrome to date, at nineteen weeks, five days between June 29 and November 13. It was a dozen years since Andrew Lloyd Webber's show, with the late TS Eliot his unwitting lyricist, had been the hit of the West End, but in some ways the wait had only served to whet the Bristol audience's appetite. Besides, prominent in the cast was the city's own Robin Cousins, showing that there was a performing life after his Olympic figure skating triumphs. Anticipating Disney's *The Lion King*, this was a show where outlandish creatures broke away from the confines of the stage to strut their stuff down the aisles to Gillian Lynne's stunning choreography. And even though everybody must have heard *Memory* a million times, there was still not a dry eye in the house when it was reprised here.

1994-95, Pickwick

Sir Harry Secombe was contemplating retirement at the age of seventy-one in 1992, but he was persuaded to reprise his role as the lead in *Pickwick – The Musical*, which had been a West End hit in the mid-Sixties and it arrived at the Hippodrome for Christmas 1994, nearly forty years after he had first appeared there as a Goon alongside Peter Sellers and Spike Milligan. Although unwell, Harry managed a barnstorming rendition of 'If I Ruled the World' every night for nearly seven weeks, and with Ruth Madoc also excelling, the show was a runaway success and took more than a million pounds at the Box Office. Apart from the 1955 Goons

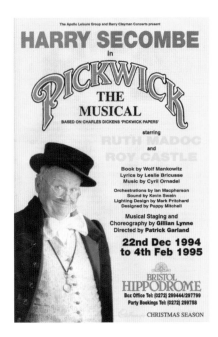

extravaganza, Harry had earlier appeared at the Hippodrome in *Rocking The Town* in 1957, *Secombe Here!* in 1963 and *Fall In, The Stars*, a one-nighter in March, 1983 in aid of the Army Benevolent Fund. In 1994 he also reminisced about a dreadful ex-servicemen's show he had appeared in at the 'Hippo' in 1948, but in fact it had been the Empire in Old Market.

1999, Phantom of the Opera

The story of this Andrew Lloyd Webber classic's stay at the Hippodrome mirrors that of his *Cats* in many ways. Both arrived in Bristol a dozen or so years after making their West End debuts, and at nineteen weeks and five days they share the theatre's all-time record run honours. With Scott Davies, Zoe Curlett and Richard Lake in the lead roles, it ran from January 5 to May 22, and when the show's twenty-seven articulated lorries rolled into town, some four million pounds had already been taken at the Box Office.

2004, Mary Poppins

There was great excitement over the world premiere of the Disney favourite *Mary Poppins*. How could it possibly emulate Julie Andrews flying over the streets of London, match the spectacular dance routines of the film – or recapture Dick Van Dyke's cockney accent? These questions were immediately answered in Disney and Sir Cameron Macintosh's wonderful production. Laura Michelle Kelly as Mary soared out over the heads of the audience in breathtaking style,

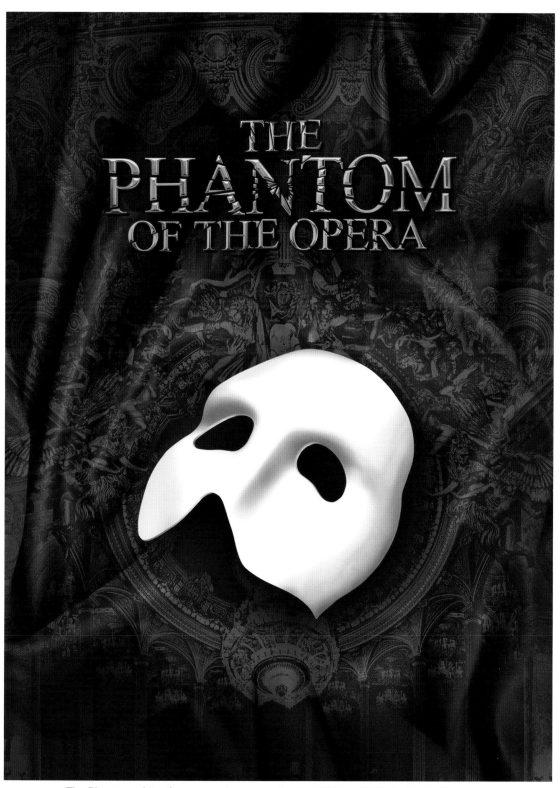

The Phantom of the Opera, brochure cover for the UK Tour, 2012. Design by Dewynters

Earl Carpenter as the Phantom and Katie Hall as Christine in 'The Music of the Night' from *The Phantom of the Opera*, UK Tour, 2012. Photograph: Michael Le Poer Trench © Cameron Mackintosh Ltd

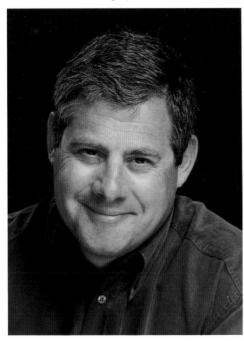

Cameron Mackintosh.
Photograph: Michael Le Poer Trench © Cameron Mackintosh Ltd

The chimney sweeps in 'Step in Time', *Mary Poppins*, Bristol, 2004. Below: Laura Michelle Kelly as Mary in *Mary Poppins*
Photographs: Michael Le Poer Trench © Cameron Mackintosh Ltd

while with her feet on the ground she joined in the many equally enthralling dance routines. That fine actor David Haig brought his own interpretation of the children's father, Mr Banks; the part had been played on film by David Tomlinson, who in the fifties had starred at the Hippodrome in the comedy *The Little Hut*.

2010, Dick Whittington

The Hippodrome's incoming General Manager Christiaan de Villiers had hardly got his feet under his desk before Barbara Windsor and the rest of the *Dick Whittington* crew breezed into town, and he and the rest of his team have only the happiest memories of the show. That applies to a good many others in Bristol, in fact, because wherever she went, Babs was

Barbara Windsor, 'a delight'

a delight, appearing here, there and everywhere to help good causes and put smiles on people's faces. On stage, this was a show that pulled out all the stops, with lavish sets, a quality script, novelties including a 3D sequence, endless music and song and sky-high production values. The star did the lot, from making her entrance as Fairy Bowbells on a wire from high above in a glittering pink dress with wings to the hilarious Lady GaGa routine, and among her support was Andy Ford, the hilarious West Country comic who has become a fixture in Hippodrome pantos in recent years.

17

A very special place

Running a top-ranking theatre in the early twenty-first century is a major undertaking, a team effort accomplished by a staff of up to a hundred and eighty working full-time and part-time in Bristol, supported by the owners The Ambassador Theatre Group's (ATG) specialists in Woking and central London. Of course it does not end there, since all the major shows come with their own technical crew, well used to and adept at working alongside the in-house team, wherever they might be. At the end of a performance, maybe it is a small handful of stars that basks in the glory and adulation, but they would not be up there doing so without a quite extraordinary joint effort by scores of talented people, day after day, night after night.

As we have noted, ATG have been at the helm since 2009, but many staff have been aboard for twenty years or longer, including the heads of all the departments. The longest-serving member is one of the Stage Door Keepers, Tony Bell, who came to the Hippodrome in 1978 and has been in his present post since 1984, but a number of his colleagues can look back to life here in the eighties. The Box Office manager, Ian Kennedy, joined the staff after leaving college in 1987, and everyone agrees that his department has probably seen more change than any other in the intervening years.

'New technology has altered everything,' he says. 'When I first joined we had ticket books and big plans and were manually writing down people's names on little squares representing seats. If we lost the ticket book or lost the plan, we were stuck. The Box Office used to be in the foyer, and we had telephonists, a core team of four, in a room below, taking incoming ticket requests. Computerisation was a gradual thing. We didn't go straight to a call centre situation. Changes really began to happen when the Box Office moved from within the theatre to where we are now. The department is smaller in terms of staff numbers, but that happens with technology. It certainly makes things easier in balancing, accounting and reporting.

'When it comes to selling tickets, we are reliant on the policy of incoming companies. These days there seems to be an eagerness amongst producers to get tickets for their shows on sale a year or more in advance. It's always a balancing act and something over which we don't always have control'.

Ian had been a student at Bristol Polytechnic, doing his course but also running the students'

A grand auditorium

union entertainments, organising discos, bands and the like. 'From there I just drifted into this,' he reflects. 'In a way it was a dream job, but it didn't pay much, and it's still not the money that keeps you here. It's the place, the people, the whole spirit of the Hippodrome. When I joined in February, 1987 it was the last week of the pantomime, and at the end of it there was a party on stage. I thought hey, this is good.' This was the year when Jim Davidson played Buttons in *Cinderella* and met Alison Holloway, the HTV presenter sent round to interview him at the start of the run. By the time Ian joined the staff the two had married – on the afternoon of the wedding Alison came to the matinee still dressed in her wedding outfit – but she did not stay the third Mrs Davidson for very long. In fact the comedian's relationship with the Hippodrome lasted a good deal longer than his with her, since he returned in panto in 1979, 1996 and 2002.

When it comes to drawing up the programme, the bulk of the work is done away from Bristol. 'Programming is now such a science, and with so many shows on the road and so many productions available, it's essential to have a central programming department,' says General Manager Christiaan de Villiers. 'Ours is based in Oxford and at Charing Cross, and it is responsible for serving all the group's forty venues. Usually what happens is that promoters contact them, and they will have each venue's diary before them, piecing together the dates like a jigsaw puzzle. Programming is a very busy and very dynamic department, but to fill forty venues every day of the year is a big task. At some times of the year there is not enough what we call 'product' to do the rounds, and it's at that time that there's a chance for local shows to come in. If there's anything regional I will start the ball rolling from this end, or contact regional programming.

'Of course, it is also a fact that some venues are more desirable to a company than others, and they become part of the bargaining process. The Hippodrome is right up there at the forefront of the group, so our programming department might say "We'll give you Bristol, but you have to go to such-a-place in February." Also, within individual venues, you have to have balance in what you put in. You don't want too many similar shows together, but musicals are so massively popular, it's not always easy to space them out. There is discussion between programming and us. We get so much returning product coming to us, they will ask our opinion. Bristol is not one of the bigger-risk venues, because we are so well supported. Because the audience is so loyal, you can almost guarantee that ninety per cent of the shows will work in Bristol. Take *The Mousetrap*. Who would think an Agatha Christie play with no big-name stars would do well in a large venue like this, but in fact it sold incredibly well in the spring of 2013. It's no wonder companies love the city, love the theatre, and I believe one of our strengths is that there is no immediate crossover of interests with other Bristol venues. We each have our own speciality, we are in constant contact with one another and relationships are good.

'Well in advance of a production coming in we send the company our spec, so that they know exactly what we can do and what we can't. Then they send us their riders (lists of requirements), but while on the day they have their own specialists in, they need our staff who know

the venue to work with them as a joint effort. Changeover periods can be frantic, with maybe a day to get one out and the next one in. Sometimes we have to hire outside staff over and above our own and the production's, just to get the crossover right. It's amazing what they can do. You walk in on a Monday morning and it looks like a Rolling Stones concert is being set up with all the gear lying around everywhere. Then you come back in the afternoon and wow, it's there. It staggers me what they can achieve in no time at all. They're so organised. With bigger shows it can take longer, but even if it takes weeks to put it in, it will only be two days to take it out.

'Then you leave here on the last Saturday night and by that stage the scenery is part of the furniture, perhaps even something you've got attached to. The people too they come and go, but you get to know and like them. Then you come in on Monday morning and for a brief spell it's all gone, the stage is just a vast blank black space, like a warehouse, and it's odd, it seems to leave an empty space in your life too – until suddenly it's all hustle and bustle and what looks like well-organised chaos, and the old place bursts back into action again.'

Way up in the gallery above the left of the stage, Head Flyman Paul Bookham oversees a world of ropes and pulleys that, superficially at least, looks as if it could have changed little over the century. Everyone who has passed along the rear of the stalls during a show will have noted electronic lighting control boards of mind-numbing complexity, yet up here, the work is still predominantly manual. At one time, the task of operating the ropes often fell to retired or off-duty sailors, which explains the old superstition that there should be no whistling backstage. On ships, mariners used to work to whistle commands, which could have caused confusion in the split-second occupation of raising and lowering scenery. As it is, the crew up there works to a board of hand-written cue instructions, along with a panel of small green lights which show when action needs to be taken. But isn't that a bit haphazard? 'Well, anyone who comes to the Hippodrome regularly will know that we don't often get it wrong,' says Paul. 'But yes, in theory, if there are several cue lights in quick succession, you only have to be distracted for a split second and you don't quite know where you're up to. Don't talk to me about the performance of *Grease* that night...'

Julian Clary in *Cinderella*, 2004

Then there are the front-of-house staff, some sixty all told, full-time, part-time and casual, from some of the oldest hands in the theatre to first-year students. 'They can get into the rhythm of a weekly show or longer, but if they get into a run of one-nighters they're absolutely shattered, having to deal with the varied audiences,' says Christiaan de Villiers. 'It's great having the experienced ones; they can read an audience, understand its demographics. Different shows bring different audiences – something for all staff to relate to'. Young or old, front-of-house staff have to be well trained these days, and showing people to their seats is a tougher job than it used to be. 'When I started here I was front-of-house, working in the bar,' says the Hippodrome's Marketing Manager, Steve Jones. 'You'd have an inspection and if you had a clean shirt on and your shoes were OK, that was it. Now there's a much more detailed brief. In my first week I did Welsh National Opera and Freddie Starr. That told me all I needed to know about what to expect in the job. Now they have to pass tests, including maths before they are taken on. They have to be generally pretty skilled. They have to know everything about the theatre.'

It was whilst working front-of-house that Stage Door Keeper Tony Bell applied for a job in 1978, when the owners were still Stoll-Moss: 'I came in for my interview and was asked to paint some chairs. At the end of it I asked if I'd passed, the chap said yes, and that was my

'That was a Hoff audience': David Hasselhoff, Andy Ford and cast, *Peter Pan* 2011

first day's work at The Bristol Hippodrome.' Since then he has become steeped in backstage lore, though he does not go out of his way to engage with the artists. 'My priority is to give them their freedom,' he insists. 'I've never been one to start talking to them, beyond what is necessary for me to do my job. Once they're here, they're here to work; that's always been one of my golden rules. I don't even collect autographs – although I've got one or two. That said, I'm the first one they come to with their problems, which often don't go beyond "How do I switch my shower on?" One Christmas a young guy in the chorus asked me if I knew of a pilot who could fly him home up north on Christmas Eve. His parents wanted him with them and they were willing to pay. I got in touch with the flying club at Bristol Airport, and left it to him. It's just local knowledge they're looking for, most of the time.'

'Ad-lib? He might as well not had a script'. Mickey Rooney in *Cinderella*, 2009

Tony is not a great one for backstage gossip, but has happy memories of two high-profile Americans, Mickey Rooney and David Hasselhoff. 'Mickey Rooney was a really nice guy, extremely funny,' he recalls. 'You never knew what he was going to do on stage or off. Ad-lib? Sometimes he might as well not have had a script. Several times, including twice in one day, he asked me to get him a taxi to take him home, because he'd had enough. I'd phone the manager, tell him Mr Rooney was asking for a taxi home, and it would always be sorted out. David Hasselhoff was fine, very Hollywood. I remember him coming off stage going "That was a Hoff audience, a Hoff audience," as if he were the only one in the show. They were real crowd-pullers, but in 1988 Engelbert Humperdinck wasn't such a big draw and made us give away tickets for his second show, rather than play to a sparse house. There were complimentaries

Ghosts

Ghost – The Musical was the Hippodrome's big late-summer attraction of 2013, but some will tell you that spooky goings-on in the theatre are not restricted to the stage. Maybe for such an atmospheric space, and one standing on medieval hospital land, it is not as over-run with tormented souls as it might have been, and there is certainly not one abiding figure that has reappeared constantly over the century.

Nevertheless, there have been two sightings in modern times. The most recent when a front-of-house supervisor whilst checking the fire exit nearest to stage right, felt uneasy and then saw the spectre of a woman in medieval clothing. On the other occasion, a customer service manager checking the stairs to the rear right of the auditorium saw the figure of a child sitting on a step – and made a speedy exit. What is it about corridors and staircases?

flying all over town. Then there was Joan Collins. I actually asked who she was when she came in. She *was* Joan Collins, but not the way you'd expect Joan Collins to look. She was a really nice lady, very down-to-earth. They'd just driven up from her house in France, none of your private jets. Then she came down from her dressing room to do her show of stories and reminiscences, and you weren't in any doubt about who she was any more.'

Many in the know say the profile of celebrity has changed over the years, and with it the stars' expectations. 'The balance has shifted from the artists to the production or tour,' says Christiaan de Villiers. 'Twenty years ago it was the celebrities who called the shots, but now it's the show. There's a level of celebrity where you can expect the riders, the special demands, but most of the time the actors who come here just want to get on with their job. Jason Donovan was here recently with the musical *Priscilla Queen Of The Desert*. He's a big name, but he made no demands whatsoever. He was in the middle of a long tour and Bristol was the place he was doing his job of work that particular fortnight. As soon as a show's in I go round to everybody to welcome them to the theatre and ensure they are all right, and I never get any kind of negative reaction. They just want a nice, clean working environment, that's all.'

Old hands on the staff look back on some odd requests over the years, but not many. Rudolf Nureyev wanted everything peach coloured in his dressing room and David Hasselhoff asked for a bed in his instead of the normal couch. Since he was living just around the corner this struck some as a bit rich, especially as he apparently never used it, anyway; but as celebrity excesses go, it scarcely registers on the Richter scale. Neither did the cast of *Joseph*'s plea for a table football game, while Shakin' Stevens's custom of organising four different fans to come in and decorate his dressing room every night – mainly with pictures of him – was usually seen as a harmless act of vanity. A lot of the time, the way in which a request was made appears to be the issue. It still rankles that Dana asked staff to call Jolly's at the Triangle in Clifton to get some shoes sent down, while Barbara Windsor's need for someone to pop round to Marks and Spencer's for her is recalled with joyful affection; everybody agrees that Babs was one of the all-time sweeties.

There has been a constant upgrading of the dressing rooms over the years, but nobody at the Hippodrome tries to present them as anything other than clean, functional workspaces that do the job for which they were designed. Back in the seventies the pop star Clodagh Rogers gave the then management a

1980: new dressing rooms arrive

wake-up call by complaining that there was no shower in her room. Today it seems a reasonable observation from someone whose job it was to go out and stand in front of two thousand people and dazzle them, and was a reminder that the days of variety, where old-timers' ritualistic grumbles about digs, dressing rooms and Sunday trains were a fact of life, were long since gone. Later, the comedy duo Cannon and Ball did not find conditions backstage particularly amusing, but further improvements since then have headed off the problems – give or take.

'I was the first one in one Boxing Day morning to get ready for the pantomime,' says Tony Bell, 'and when I turned on the lights up to the dressing rooms it was pop-pop-pop-pop. I started walking up the stairs only to be met by water rushing down. Some water tanks in the dressing rooms had fallen over, and all hell was let loose as we dashed around getting the costumes out of the wet and trying to make the place habitable again.' It ended up with the children in the cast changing on stage – but of course, the show went on.

Tony's Stage Door domain still looks like something out of some old Hollywood showbiz

The Ascot scene in *My Fair Lady*, UK Tour, 2006.
Photograph: Michael Le Poer Trench © Cameron Mackintosh Ltd

Amy Nuttall as Eliza in *My Fair Lady*, UK Tour, 2006.
Photograph: Michael Le Poer Trench © Cameron
Mackintosh Ltd

musical; for instance, surely those A to Z mail pigeonholes behind his desk are redundant in this age of texts and emails? 'You'd be surprised,' he says. 'The big opening nights can still have mail flooding in by the sackful. On the opening night of *Mary Poppins* we started counting the packages coming in for the cast and stopped at a hundred and sixty – flowers, chocolate and champagne. And that's before the Hippodrome and the production company gave the stars their welcome gift. More recently, fax congratulations for Disney's *The Lion King* came in from all over the world. It can be manic, but it's a nice old-fashioned tradition, seeing the flowers coming in. Less nice to see them abandoned in the dressing rooms, of course, and that's when we get a taxi and send them to hospitals. Teddy bears and soft toys go to the children's hospital.'

As the longest-serving member of staff, Tony Bell strives to put into words what it means to him and others to work here: 'The stars come and go, but this place goes on and on. Any company can own the Hippodrome, but we always feel that we work for the Hippodrome, rather than its owners. Once you've been here for a while, it really does get into your veins. We're like a family.'

The final word, however, must go to General Manager Christiaan de Villiers. 'This grand old lady is a hundred years old, but she is still at the top of her game,' he says. 'She can take in any show that comes out of the West End, and to do that you need to invest backstage, not just in the dressing rooms but in stage facilities, as well as keeping front of house up to the mark. It's an ongoing process, and what makes it tougher is that because we're so busy, forty-nine weeks a year, it's hard to find the dark time to do it in. What has not changed over the years, though, is that we believe, as Oswald Stoll believed, that Bristol deserves the very best. Whether you've been here once or a hundred times, this place makes some kind of impact on you which you never seem to forget. Coming from South Africa, working in various venues and then arriving here in Bristol, I've never before experienced the feeling of absolute owner-ship the people here have for this theatre. It's not that it's publicly owned in a literal sense, but it's a pride that I've never remotely seen before. To me, that's what makes both the Hippodrome and the city it's proud to serve, a very special place.'

Premieres

The Bristol Hippodrome has staged many productions that
could be described as premieres in a limited sense, but among
the most significant are:

British, *Guys and Dolls*, 1953
European, *The Music Man*, 1961
European, *Sail Away*, 1962
British, *Jeeves*, 1975
World, *Windy City*, 1982
World, *The Nutcracker*, English National Ballet, 2002
World, *Mary Poppins*, 2004

Harry Stott (Michael), Laura Michelle Kelly (Mary), Melanie La Barrie (Mrs Corry), Gavin Lee (Bert), Charlotte
Spencer (Jane), Claire Machin (Miss Lark) in 'Supercalafragalistic', *Mary Poppins*, Bristol, 2004
Photograph: Michael Le Poer Trench © Cameron Mackintosh Ltd

Record runs

1= *Cats* June 29-November 13, 1993 (19 weeks, 5 days)

1= *Phantom of the Opera* January 5-May 22, 1999 (19 weeks, 5 days)

3 *My Fair Lady* April 4-August 15, 1964 (19 weeks, 1 day)

4 *Beauty And The Beast* December 7, 2001-March 23, 2002 (15 weeks, 2 days)

5 *Mother Goose* December 22, 1977-April 1, 1978 (14 weeks, 3 days)

6= *Aladdin* December 22, 1980-March 28, 1981 (14 weeks)

6= *Annie* December 21, 1981-March 27, 1982 (14 weeks)

8 *Miss Saigon* February 6-May 10, 2003 (13 weeks, 3 days)

9 *Chitty Chitty Bang Bang* March 9-June 9, 2007 (13 weeks, 2 days)

10 *Les Misérables* December 29, 1997-March 28, 1998 (13 weeks)

INDEX

Illustrations are indicated by the page number in **bold**

Here are a few big thank you's

To Gerry Parker and John Hudson – you would not be reading
this book without them

To John Sansom and Clara Hudson at Redcliffe Press Ltd and
Stephen Morris – thank you for persevering with such novices in
the publishing world. We got there in the end

To Jess Cox for her assistance with the photographic placement
and Zoe Parker for her help with the background research

To Ian Kennedy, Box Office Manager for his diligence,
knowledge and all round unfailing enthusiasm for this project

To all the stars, cast, musicians, producers, creatives and crew
who make the magic on stage happen

To all the unsung heroes (otherwise known as the theatre staff)
for being such trusted custodians of this theatre

To the wonderful loyal audiences – without whom The Bristol
Hippodrome would not continue to go from strength to
strength

And last but most certainly not least, to the grand old lady
herself for being such a magnificent home to so many
productions over the past 100 years and long into the future.
Long may she reign